Testing Practitioner Handbook

Gain insights into the latest technology and business trends within testing domains

Renu Rajani

BIRMINGHAM - MUMBAI

Testing Practitioner Handbook

First published: March 2017

Production reference: 1170317

Published by Packt Publishing Ltd.
Livery Place
35 Livery Street
Birmingham B3 2PB, UK.

ISBN 978-1-78829-954-1

www.packtpub.com

Credits

Author
Renu Rajani

Reviewer
Jorge Armin Garcia Lopez

Commissioning Editor
Ashwin Nair

Acquisition Editor
Denim Pinto

Content Development Editor
Anurag Ghogre

Technical Editor
Rutuja Vaze

Copy Editor
Shaila Kusanale

Proofreader
Safis Editing

Indexer
Tejal Daruwale Soni

Graphics
Abhinash Sahu

Production Coordinator
Deepika Naik

About the Author

Renu Rajani is a seasoned IT services/consulting leader with 27 years of experience. She has worked with reputed tier-1 IT services companies. Renu's experience spans across delivery, transformation, providing technical solutions, outsourcing governance, and consulting.

She has served Tier-1 organizations including IBM, Citi, Capgemini, KPMG Consulting in key leadership roles.

Renu is an active blogger on digital quality assurance, technology, and managed services and has a follower base of over 15K on social media. She has been a key contributor to Capgemini/Sogeti/HPE World Quality Report during 2015-17. She has led the creation of go-to-market offerings in the area of digital, DevOps, and business assurance.

Renu has been recipient of the *Testing Thought Leadership* award in 2008 by PureTesting and *Testing Leader* of the year award by Unicom in 2015.

This book brings together some of her popular blogs on latest technologies and QA considerations in a book form. Renu authored her first book on software testing in 2003 with McGrawHill.

Renu holds an MS from the Krannert Graduate School of Management, Purdue University USA, an MBA in Finance from DAVV Indore, and a B Tech in Computer Science from IET, Lucknow University. She is an IBM Sr PM certified with DPE/SM discipline, and holds the ITIL V3, CAIIB, and PMP Certifications.

Acknowledgement

I would like to thank my family for putting up with my blogging/social media activities that I have been deeply entrenched into and have led to this book. I would like to thank several colleagues who have contributed to the authoring of my blogs. A list of contributors for the supporting content of respective chapters is provided in the following table:

Contributors Name	Chapter Number
Vamsi Venkata Ch	39
Sripriya CP	6, 45
Ranganath Gomatham	16, 17, 18, 19, 20, 36
Manish Goyal	7,8, 10, 14, 32
Sabyasachi Guharay	30, 44
Sunil Hs	15
Vaishali Jayade	27
Varun Khanna	38, 45
Sharad Kumar	24
Pulkit Mathur	12, 31, 33, 34, 35
Jyotirmay Mishra	15
Sumanth Murthy	22
Manojkumar Nagaraj	4, 26, 29, 37, 42
Vidya Prasanna	9
Vishal Rai	29
Rohit Sharan	2, 5
Prashanth SP	13
Shyam Sridhar	3
Palaniappan Subramanian	38
Mukund Thaker	39,40
Rajesh Thakker	41
Ashish Velankar	25
Bhaskar Venkataraman	21, 26

About the Reviewer

Jorge Armin Garcia Lopez is a very passionate Information Security Consultant from Mexico with more than 8 years of experience in computer security, penetration testing, intrusion detection/prevention, malware analysis, and incident response. He is the head of GCS-CERT. He is also a security researcher at Cipher Storm Ltd Group and is the cofounder and CEO of the most important security conference in Mexico, called BUGCON. He holds important security industry certifications, such as OSCP, GCIA, and GPEN. He loves to review code and books about information security and programming languages. He has worked on *Penetration Testing with Blackbox*, *Penetration Testing with the Bash Shell*, *Learning OpenStack Networking (Neutron)*, *Django Essentials*, and *Getting Started with Djando* all by Packt.

www.PacktPub.com

eBooks, discount offers, and more

Did you know that Packt offers eBook versions of every book published, with PDF and ePub files available? You can upgrade to the eBook version at www.PacktPub.com and as a print book customer, you are entitled to a discount on the eBook copy. Get in touch with us at customercare@packtpub.com for more details.

At www.PacktPub.com, you can also read a collection of free technical articles, sign up for a range of free newsletters and receive exclusive discounts and offers on Packt books and eBooks.

https://www.packtpub.com/mapt

Get the most in-demand software skills with Mapt. Mapt gives you full access to all Packt books and video courses, as well as industry-leading tools to help you plan your personal development and advance your career.

Why subscribe?

- Fully searchable across every book published by Packt
- Copy and paste, print, and bookmark content
- On demand and accessible via a web browser

Customer Feedback

Thanks for purchasing this Packt book. At Packt, quality is at the heart of our editorial process.

If you'd like to join our team of regular reviewers, you can e-mail us at customerreviews@packtpub.com. We award our regular reviewers with free eBooks and videos in exchange for their valuable feedback. Help us be relentless in improving our products!

Table of Contents

Preface

The book is based on my experience of leading and transforming large test engagements and architecting solutions for customer testing requirements, bids, or problem areas. I have been actively blogging in the area of *Managed Testing Services*, various emerging technologies in the digital world, and how these impact the way quality assurance is carried out.

My continued blogging activity over the last two years, and the inputs and encouragement from my follower base have encouraged me to author this Quality Assurance (QA) practitioners handbook. With each blogpost, I provided a point of view on emerging areas before others.

This book would help QA and other IT professionals keep abreast of industry and technology changes and better adapt to digital transformation. This book would be a valuable source to find points of view, practices, trends, tools, and solutions for QA professionals involved in new-age testing.

What this book covers

Chapter 1, State of Digital Transformation – What Has Changed in the Last Four Years (2013-16)? to *Chapter 5, Crowdsourcing – Enabling Flexible, On-Demand Testing COEs*: We start with trends in digital transformation in *Chapter 1, State of Digital Transformation – What Has Changed in the Last Four Years (2013-16)?*. Through *Chapter 2, Future of Testing Engagement Models – Are Predictions of Increased QA Spends Justified?*, to *Chapter 5, Crowdsourcing – Enabling Flexible, On-Demand Testing COEs*, we cover the evolution of testing engagement and operating models such as Managed Services, Testing Center of Excellence (TCOE), Digital Factory QA Model, crowd sourcing, weekend testing, and various value levers available through emerging QA engagement operating models.

Chapter 6, Testing Goes an Extra Mile over Weekends, to *Chapter 20, Accessibility Test Automation in DevOps Environment,* cover testing and automation in Agile/DevOps engagements, covering functional and non-functional (performance, TDM, Test Environment Management, virtualization, and so on) areas. The following are covered in these chapters:

- Testing in Agile/DevOps engagements, Trends in agile adoption, (*Chapters 6, Testing Goes an Extra Mile over Weekends* to *Chapter 8, Agile and DevOps Adoption are Gaining Momentum*).

- We will cover how agile and DevOps complement each other in *Chapter 9, Does the Rise of DevOps Undermine Agile?*

- We discuss the role of automation in DevOps life cycle, present a framework, and analyze the spending in QA as against design, development, and production support. We will cover how agile and DevOps complement each other in *Chapter 10, Role of Automation in DevOps Life Cycle,* we present a method to assess the state of DevOps adoption through a baselining and benchmarking approach

- *Chapter 11, Assessing State of Your DevOps Adoption with DevOps Benchmarking Approach,* we present a method to assess the state of DevOps adoption through a baselining and benchmarking approach.

- *Chapter 12, Accelerating DevOps – ChatOps Is the New Cool* covers Chat-Ops, an emerging technique to collaborate/communicate in the DevOps environment

- *Chapter 13, Behavior-Driven Development (BDD) Using Gherkin in Agile/ DevOps Environment* covers Behavior-Driven Development (BDD), a tool (for example, Gherkin) to script in an English-like language, and the basic features of Gherkin

- *Chapter 14, Automating Configuration Management for DevOps Test Environments* covers automating in DevOps life cycle, for example, automating configuration management

- *Chapter 15, Automated Test Data Management in the DevOps Environment* covers microservice architecture

- *Chapter 16, Testing in DevOps Life Cycle Using Microservices Architecture* covers test environments

- *Chapter 17, Automated Test Environments for DevOps* covers automating in DevOps life cycle, for example, automating configuration management

- In *Chapter 18, Service Virtualization as an Enabler of DevOps,* we cover service virtualization as an enabler of DevOps

- *Chapter 19, Best Practices in Identifying Regression Test Cases* covers guidelines and best practices in identifying regression test cases

- *Chapter 19, Accessibility Test Automation in DevOps Environment* covers automating accessibility tests

- *Chapter 20, Accessibility Test Automation in DevOps Environment* covers test automation in DevOps enviornment

Chapter 21, Performance Tuning of Java Applications to *Chapter 34, Blockchain Technology – Assuring Secure Business* cover the trends in social media, mobility, analytics, and cloud (SMAC) applications, and the QA considerations for these. The key trends and QA considerations pertain to the following:

- *Chapter 21, Performance Tuning of Java Applications* discusses the need for performance tuning in digital applications and covers tuning using Java utilities for Java applications

- *Chapter 22, Testing Mobile Applications – Key Challenges and Considerations* covers mobile applications

- *Chapter 23, Testing Analytics Applications – What Has Changed in SMAC World* covers analytics applications

- *Chapter 24, Migrating Applications to Cloud Environments – Key Testing Considerations* covers covers migration to the cloud

- *Chapter 25, How Should a Tester Adapt to Cloud – Call for Change of Mindset among Testers* calls for a change of mindset, which is needed for testing applications in the cloud, and the need to understand and prepare for the distance, break communication barriers, application security, platform replication, and the use of appropriate tools

- *Chapter 26, On-Demand Performance Testing on Self-Service Environments* presents performance testing as a service framework with built-in tools, data management, and environments in the cloud for cloud and enterprise applications

- *Chapter 27, Quality Assurance for Digital Marketing Initiatives* presents digital marketing as one of the emerging applications in the digital revolution and QA considerations for the readiness of content, media, and messaging involved in digital marketing applications

- *Chapter 28, Security Dashboard for the Board* emphasizes the importance of securing IT in a digital world and board-level attention being placed on the topic. A security dashboard for the board is presented

Chapter 29, Applying Robotic Automation to Mobile Applications Testing to *Chapter 35, Technologies for Digital Supply Chains and QA Considerations* cover futuristic technologies, IoT, machine learning, cognitive applied to the business, and how the QA discipline is preparing to test for these technologies and apply these in testing:

- *Chapter 29, Applying Robotic Automation to Mobile Applications Testing* covers the application of robotics technologies to test mobile applications
- *Chapter 30, Key Considerations in Testing Internet of Things (IoT) Applications* covers covers the key considerations in testing IoT applications
- *Chapter 31, Algorithmic Business – In Need of Model-Based Testing* discusses businesses being driven by algorithms and introduces *Algorithmic Business* and how *Model-based Testing* is leveraged in these businesses
- *Chapter 32, Making Testing Adaptive, Interactive, Iterative, and Contextual with Cognitive Intelligence* covers applying cognitive intelligence to testing in order to carry out testing in an adaptive, interactive, iterative, and contextual manner
- *Chapter 33, FinTech – A New Disruptor in Industry and Implications for Testing and QA* presents FinTech as a disrupter in the Financial Services industry and the QA considerations for this
- *Chapter 34, Blockchain Technology – Assuring Secure Business* presents Blockchains to assure a secured business and the QA considerations
- *Chapter 35, Technologies for Digital Supply Chains and QA Considerations* presents the upcoming technologies in the supply chain domain (connected autonomous vehicles, drones, AR/VR, 3D printing), and the QA considerations

Chapter 36, Potential Innovations in eHealth-Care – Implications for Testing and QA to *Chapter 41, Testing Airline Digital Applications – Case for Responsive Design* covers specific domains—how digital transformation is impacting these domains, specific business challenges, QA challenges, and a way to address them. Specific industries/domains covered include e-healthcare:

- *Chapter 36, Potential Innovations in eHealth-Care – Implications for Testing and QA* covers testing and QA implications
- *Chapter 37, Trends in the Global Automotive Sector – Implications for Testing and QA*, covers consumer products and retail
- *Chapter 38, Digital Transformation in Consumer Products and Retail Sector – QA Considerations* covers Energy and Utilities
- *Chapter 39, Digital Transformation Trends in Energy and Utilities – QA Considerations* covers Smart Meters and Smart Grids

- *Chapter 40, Smart Energy and Smart Grids – In Need of Effective Testing* covers Airlines
- *Chapter 41, Testing Airline Digital Applications – Case for Responsive Design* covers testing airline digital applications.

Chapter 42, Orthogonal Array Testing (OAT) – an Application in Healthcare Industry to *Chapter 46, Robotics and Machine Learning Combined with Internet of Things – What Could This Mean for Indian Services Industries* conclude the book with four chapters on the impact of digital transformation, robotics, machine learning, IoT, and other emerging technologies presented in this book on IT, consulting, and testing:

- *Chapter 42, Orthogonal Array Testing (OAT) – an Application in Healthcare Industry* we will discuss challenges facing the H&LS industry, the need for robust testing, and use of the Orthogonal Array Testing (OAT) technique to optimize testing, and use of the OAT tool
- *Chapter 43, Future of Consulting in the Era of Digital Disruption* covers the future of the consulting industry
- *Chapter 44, Future of Testing in the Digital World* covers the future of testing
- *Chapter 45, Future of Testing – Career Opportunities* covers the future of testing careers in the face of a digital transformation
- *Chapter 46, Robotics and Machine Learning Combined with Internet of Things – What Could This Mean for Indian Services Industries* concludes with a point of view on what robotics and machine learning, combined with IoT, have in store for the future of the services industry

What you need for this book

There are no supplementary aids in addition to this book.

Who this book is for

This book is meant for practicing population in QA and testing area, but other professionals in IT services and businesses would equally benefit. It covers the latest trends and practices that testing and QA professionals should keep abreast of, given the advancements in digital technologies. The book does not contain the basics of testing that a QA professional practices in daily life, for example, how to write a test plan or test case, and so on.

Conventions

In this book, you will find a number of text styles that distinguish between different kinds of information. Here are some examples of these styles and an explanation of their meaning.

Code words in text, database table names, folder names, filenames, file extensions, pathnames, dummy URLs, user input, and Twitter handles are shown as follows: " we can use `this.gender == FEMALE;` instead of `this.gender.equals("Female");`."

A block of code is set as follows:

```
Boolean t1 = new Boolean (true);
System.out.println(t1=!Boolean.TRUE);
System.out.println(t1.==(Boolean.TRUE));
produces the output: False OR True
```

New terms and **important words** are shown in bold. Words that you see on the screen, for example, in menus or dialog boxes, appear in the text like this: "After logging in, the user can navigate to **Test Centre**."

Reader feedback

Feedback from our readers is always welcome. Let us know what you think about this book—what you liked or disliked. Reader feedback is important for us as it helps us develop titles that you will really get the most out of.

To send us general feedback, simply e-mail `feedback@packtpub.com`, and mention the book's title in the subject of your message.

If there is a topic that you have expertise in and you are interested in either writing or contributing to a book, see our author guide at `www.packtpub.com/authors`.

Customer support

Now that you are the proud owner of a Packt book, we have a number of things to help you to get the most from your purchase.

Errata

Although we have taken every care to ensure the accuracy of our content, mistakes do happen. If you find a mistake in one of our books—maybe a mistake in the text or the code—we would be grateful if you could report this to us. By doing so, you can save other readers from frustration and help us improve subsequent versions of this book. If you find any errata, please report them by visiting `http://www.packtpub.com/submit-errata`, selecting your book, clicking on the **Errata Submission Form** link, and entering the details of your errata. Once your errata are verified, your submission will be accepted and the errata will be uploaded to our website or added to any list of existing errata under the Errata section of that title.

To view the previously submitted errata, go to `https://www.packtpub.com/books/content/support` and enter the name of the book in the search field. The required information will appear under the **Errata** section.

Piracy

Piracy of copyrighted material on the Internet is an ongoing problem across all media. At Packt, we take the protection of our copyright and licenses very seriously. If you come across any illegal copies of our works in any form on the Internet, please provide us with the location address or website name immediately so that we can pursue a remedy.

Please contact us at `copyright@packtpub.com` with a link to the suspected pirated material.

We appreciate your help in protecting our authors and our ability to bring you valuable content.

Questions

If you have a problem with any aspect of this book, you can contact us at `questions@packtpub.com`, and we will do our best to address the problem.

1

State of Digital Transformation – What Has Changed in the Last Four Years (2013-16)?

The year 2015 was the first time significant trends in digital transformation were spotted in the **World Quality Report (WQR)**. The upward trend continued in 2016 with the growing adoption of digital. In this chapter, we have will discuss the specific changes we witnessed in the last 4 years in QA transformation. Some of the trends I have observed are discussed further on.

Renewed focus on efficiency and effectiveness

In the last 4 years, the focus of QA transformation has evolved from centralizing QA to focus on the increased use of **Social Media, Mobility, Analytics and Cloud (SMAC)** and digital initiatives to improved customer experience.

In 2015, security and protecting corporate image were cited as the key IT objectives in line with an organization's desire to secure their digital presence and reduce the damage to their corporate reputation.

In 2016, the key strategic IT drivers included security, customer experience, and corporate image. Additionally, there was renewed focus on efficiency and effectiveness as important QA and testing objectives.

QA and testing transformation focus

The focus of the QA transformation agenda has undergone a shift over the last few years from focus on centralizing QA to addressing vulnerabilities in digital business, to increased QA spends, to increased customer, and user experience combined with security and a renewed focus on efficiency. Refer to the following table:

2013	2014	2015	2016
Centralizing and streamlining testing functions indicating continuing maturing of the QA function.	• Digital business transformation programs using SMAC technologies and Internet of Things (IoT) changed the focus and importance of QA and testing. • Focus on addressing vulnerabilities— network performance, security, and cloud service availability.	• Organizations that are more mature and advanced in digital transformation spend the most in QA and testing and have established a direct connection between quality and achieving business outcomes. • Focus of testing on usability, customer experience, and performance.	• The strategic IT drivers include security, customer experience, and corporate image. • In addition, there is a renewed focus on efficiency and effectiveness.

QA and testing transformation drivers

The key driver for QA and testing transformation has changed from cost optimization in 2013 to the need for instant access to information in 2014, to focusing on customer value and end user experience in 2015. Customer experience has stayed the focus in 2016 as well:

2013	2014	2015	2016
Cost optimization	People's need for instant connectivity and access to information	Focus on customer value and the impact of IT quality on end user experience	Protect corporate image and enhance customer experience

State of digital maturity

We define digital maturity based on whether an organization has appointed or is in the process of appointing a **Chief Digital Officer (CDO)**. The year 2016 has seen the automotive (76% respondents mention having a CDO or in the process of appointing one) and public sectors (73%) at the top of the leaderboard in digital maturity based on this criteria. These sectors had been laggards in 2015. Increased adoption of digital for citizen services and inclusion justifies the top rank for the public sector.

Spends for digital QA

About 63% of the QA budget (versus 53% in 2015) is used in QA for new developments in mobile, cloud, **Business Intelligence (BI)/Business Analytics (BA)**, and IoT areas.

There is less correlation between digital maturity and QA spend in 2016. Organizations with the absence of a digital strategy seem to have a higher QA spend than the ones with digital maturity. Why do organizations with digital strategy have lower QA spend? It is likely that in a hurry to move ahead in digital transformation, organizations have progressed in development with inadequate QA.

Predictions on the level of cloud-based applications

Cloud-based applications are set to increase over the next 3 years. There has been an overall drop in the use of the public, private, and hybrid cloud. However, the use of on premise cloud has seen a significant increase.

A surprise finding is that despite the data privacy concerns, the use of public and hybrid cloud has increased in Europe.

Also, the findings suggest that focus on functional validation while migrating to the cloud was ignored and only performance testing was considered adequate. This again suggests that in a hurry to progress in digital transformation, organizations have ignored quality.

Increased challenges in mobile and IoT multichannel testing

In 2016, the WQR findings suggest increased challenges in mobile, IoT, and multichannel testing in all the categories:

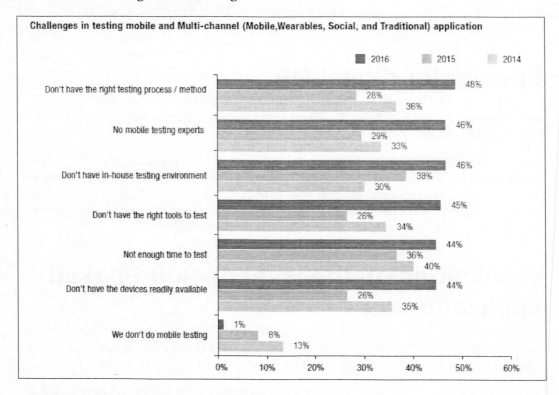

The challenge areas probed are as follows:

- Lack of right testing process or method
- Lack of experts
- Lack of an in-house test environment
- Lack of the right tools
- Inadequate time spent
- Lack of device availability to test

It is difficult to accept that there can be increased challenges given that digital has matured since 2015. The possible reasons for increased challenges could be the sheer size and complexity of digital transformation.

Reduction in customer experience testing challenges

In 2016, there was a decline cited for all the challenge areas relating to customer experience testing, namely, the following ones:

- Designing the test cases
- Implementing test tools
- Establishing test data
- Identifying end user expectations
- Establishing environments
- Getting the right coverage
- Identifying the systems
- Apps to be covered

Refer to the following graph:

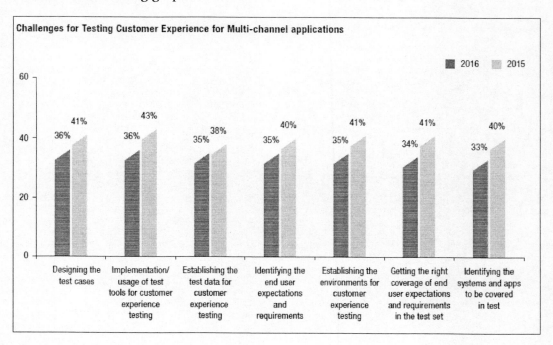

Conclusion

Is QA transformation dependent on the existence of a central **Testing Center of Excellence (TCOE)**? With increased use of SMAC technologies, organizations started abandoning centralized TCOE model in 2015 in pursuit of agile delivery models and focused on customer experience and business assurance.

Do we conclude that we witness that quality is ignored in digital transformation initiatives? Otherwise, do we conclude that quality is so embedded in digital transformations that there is a less specific need for quality? Given the evidence of increased challenges cited in 2016 in mobile, IoT, and multichannel applications, we will say there indeed is a decline in quality. The organizations will soon realize the need for focus on quality or pay the price.

For an in-depth look at the key trends in testing and QA, download the World Quality Report 2016 from `http://ow.ly/PvMd304ynId`.

2

Future of Testing Engagement Models – Are Predictions of Increased QA Spends Justified?

In this chapter, we will discuss the future of testing engagement models in light of current developments in digital space and increased adoption of Agile/DevOps models.

Would Dev-Ops shrink the amount of testing that is done in current world? If so, what would be the impact? As per WQR2016 findings, testing spend would increase up to 40% by organizations. How does this increased spend prediction align to the fact that more engagements would follow decentralized QA in Agile/DevOps life cycle?

How is QA effort spread

Let's discuss the following topics:

- How QA effort is split between development and production support
- Reasons for increase of QA effort in the design phase

Split of QA effort between development and production support

Share of QA spend in new development projects (as against enhancements/ maintenance projects) has grown from 2012-13 to 2013-14 to 2014-15, from 41% to 46% to 52% respectively.

In 2015-16, the QA spend was split 50:50 between new development and production support.

In 2014-15, for the first time, the QA spend for Development exceeded the QA spend for production support. This is in line with more development projects with organizations undertaking more digital transformation related development work. Refer to the following graph:

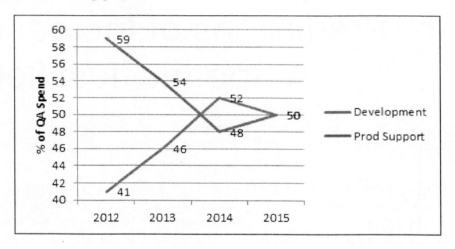

Increased QA efforts for new development – point of view

It is evident that when QA is done for new code (as against QA for maintaining/ enhancing the existing code), QA effort will be higher.

Organizations are practicing Agile/DevOps to achieve cycle time reduction (faster time to production or achieving time to market objective to gain competitive advantage) and not necessarily with a QA cost reduction objective. If code is released more often and tested in shorter cycles, one will achieve the objective of cycle time, and not necessarily cost reduction.

Continuous integration and continuous deployment are practiced. One can't integrate or deploy less-tested faulty code, so continuous testing means more iterations of testing.

The testers are carrying out executions up until production deployment and in live environment aligning to extreme right. Analysts, such as **Forrester** and **Gartner**, recommend not only *shift-left* to test early in life cycle, but also shift-right to extend tester involvement till deployment.

Increase of QA effort in the design phase

2014-15 WQR report highlighted an increased involvement of QA in high-level design phase to 14% (as against 6% in the previous year).

What is being achieved by QA involvement in the design phase?

Increased QA effort in the design phase – point of view

Shift-left practices are being leveraged to have testers contribute their domain expertise in the design phase.

In line with the trend of continuous testing to support continuous integration and deployment, there is increased automation in silo phases of test design and development (to match the software design phase).

With automated tools supporting test models and test script generation, and their integration with automated test execution, reporting and deployment tools have further pushed the shift left practice to the requirement phase.

This increase of the test effort in the design phase is being debated. It will make testing function costly. However, based on the ROIs, it can be argued that more QA effort spent in the early design phase will reduce manual interventions and reworks in later phases in the life cycle; reducing the cycle time of QA and the cost of testing in turn.

QA organizations would follow hybrid QA teams (centralized and decentralized)

In this section, we will discuss the future organization of QA teams.

As per WQR2015, the use of internal independent industrialized test TCOE stabilized and would see decline.

Use of a combination of centralized and decentralized teams (Hybrid) for QA grew from 35% in 2013-14 to 43% in 2014-15.

WQR 2015 reported 24% respondents citing plans to have internal TCOE as against 24% in 2014-15 and 23% in 2013-14.

A total of 18% cited no plan for TCOE in 2015-16 as against 20% in 2014-15 and 26% in 2013-14.

A total of 11% cited plans to use third-party TCOE in 2015-16, as against 15% in 2014-15 and 19% in 2013-14.

Trend towards Hybrid QA teams – point of view

The preceding observations point to a need for testers to work with developers through life cycle – shift-left as well as shift-right. Use of dedicated TCOEs will not continue to rise as in the past and shall need to scale to provide services in platform as service model.

In the future, we will see a cross-functional team leveraging the automated toolsets optimally to push the tested functions into production leveraging DevOps Enablers (Continuous Planning, Continuous Integration, Continuous Testing, Continuous Deployment, Continuous Monitoring, and Continuous Improvements) to deliver a highly performing system yet reducing the time to market considerably.

A tester will be expected to be aware of the functional details and help a developer by isolating the bugs to the extent of pointing to the line of code, indexing structure of the database, and pin-pointing the infrastructure that is becoming the bottleneck in meeting business objectives.

What will be the future of testing engagement models?

Analysts, such as Forrester, believe that traditional **Managed Test Services (MTS)** deals may be fewer in the future.

Recent Gartner Research findings suggest that MTS market will see a 15% growth. Organizations that are yet to mature in rolling out managed testing functions shall need to look at establishing an MTS organization while the organizations that have MTS organizations or equivalent need to look at **Managed Test Operation (MTO)** with aim to mature testing functions to Quality Assurance.

There is little doubt that organizations specializing in quality/test service offerings are looking at ways to align their models to client needs.

Both the providers as well as the clients are contemplating on the following questions:

- **Provider Perspective**: What do our clients need? What are we offering?
- **Client Perspective**: What do I need? What do I want my providers to offer?

Future of testing engagement models – point of view

Providers as well as clients have three plateaus in their businesses. I describe these plateaus in the following points:

- **Business As Usual (BAU) Plateau**: Clients want to keep lights on for a section of their BAU portfolios and manage their legacy applications to continue to service customers. Many of these engagements have QA & Testing *embedded* into the maintenance/enhancement projects. As we discussed earlier, given the higher split of QA effort in new digital transformation engagements, the share of QA effort in BAU maintenance/ production support engagements has continued to shrink over the last few years. IT service providers have addressed this plateau with the Test Factory model to pool test for many engagements, with an ability to offer continuation of knowledge, availability of tools, centralized governance and capability planning, and service based on work delivered rather than continuing dedicated practitioners for engagements during lean periods.

- **Industrialize Plateau**: Clients want to industrialize their testing, get cost advantage, and route the savings from this segment to be able to spend it for new initiatives. Testing is easier to separate out as a validation step through the life cycle to be carried out by dedicated test practitioners, using the best of the process, methods, and tooling, and offering QA services to meet the agreed SLAs/KPIs. IT service providers have addressed this plateau with MTS to industrialize the manner in which the testing service is offered cost effectively. Managed test services leverage offshore, core/flex, process and tool assets, and transformational levers to carry out testing in an industrialized manner. Testing can be carried out in agile/Devops engagements remotely through the *distributed agile* method and Managed Test Services can be Agile-MTS with a flavor of distributed Agile. Distributed Agile has been discussed in Chapter 6, *Testing goes an Extra Mile over Weekends*. What is considered *Innovative* and *Specialised* today, needs to be offered as *Industrialized* in the future, and will soon become BAU in our fast evolving IT landscape. Refer to the following diagram:

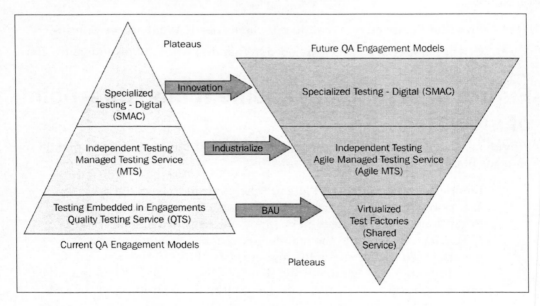

- **Innovate Plateau**: Clients need to address to digital business and be present in multiple-modes—offline, online, and multiple speeds to cater to varied customer segments. Gartner Research refers to this as bimodal IT. Speed does not always come without cost. Clients seek specialized services (for example, new developments in agile/DevOps mode) based on their needs. To address this segment, customers need business assurance (for example. assurance of time to production, time to market, and reduced failures). High quality and timeliness are most important for this plateau. Cost reduction, while a relevant need, may not be addressed for this segment due to time pressures. Providers have addressed this need of *Innovate Plateau* with *Specialised Test Services* to cater to the QA need of agile/DevOps Testing with leading-edge automation tools, business assurance to partner with clients to reduce risk in the journey, and share the risks and rewards through agreed rewards and penalties.

DevOps mind

Would DevOps shrink the amount of testing? Are Predictions on increasing QA spends justified?

DevOps is actually spreading testing across the software development life cycle. The builds are smaller and so are the QA life cycles. There are continued multiple builds though offering advantage of speed, which does not necessarily mean less QA or lesser QA spend. With new development projects on the rise for digital transformation projects, overall QA spends will be on the rise. One of the challenges to address will be to achieve a balance of the triple objectives (time, cost, and quality) in the evolving QA/DevOps world.

Conclusion

In this chapter, we considered data points about an increased split of QA effort in development projects as against production support. This aligns with the need for more QA in new development projects associated with digital transformation. We also considered the trend of increased QA effort in the design phase, which aligns with the need for Shift-Left and Shift-Right principles in the DevOps life cycle.

We considered data points relating to the future of centralized with regard to the decentralized models of QA and concluded that the future will see the use of hybrid models. Organizations will continue to use MTS and Centralized COEs for business as usual functions to carry out QA efficiently. For the digital transformation initiatives and projects in the Agile/DevOps life cycle, the projects will carry out testing in the decentralized mode. Distributed Agile is an option that is also considered.

We then discussed future testing engagement models with a 3-plateau approach to business and IT— BAU, Industrialize, and Innovate. The providers as well as clients operate in each of the three plateaus. With digital transformation on the rise, it is expected that the current pyramid of three plateaus may get reversed in favor of more *innovate* engagements and less BAU.

References

- Gartner
- Forrester
- Capgemini Sogeti HPE World Quality Report

3

The Benefits of Replacing Testing Subcontractors with Managed Testing Services

Managed Testing Services (MTS) has seen an aggressive growth in the IT industry. MTS contracts have various transformation levers. Often, customers who frequently use direct subcontractors do not think of outsourcing. For them, the very first transformational step could be to consider replacing direct contractors with outsourcing involving an outsourcing service provider.

Findings from the World Quality Report 2016 on industrialization and testing centers of excellence

The Capgemini World Quality Report 2016 #WQR2016 pointed towards a shift in intelligence-led test COEs. 49% of participants cite leveraging or increasing their managed services model with an expert QA vendor.

Refer to the following graph:

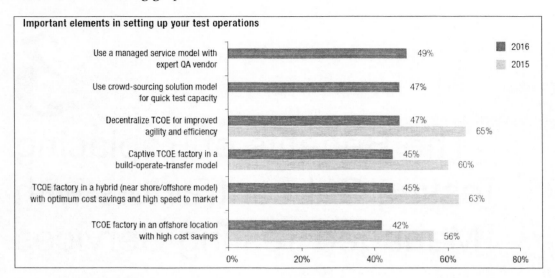

Important elements in setting up your test operations

Use a managed service model with expert QA vendor — 49% (2016)
Use crowd-sourcing solution model for quick test capacity — 47% (2016)
Decentralize TCOE for improved agility and efficiency — 47% (2016), 65% (2015)
Captive TCOE factory in a build-operate-transfer model — 45% (2016), 60% (2015)
TCOE factory in a hybrid (near shore/offshore model) with optimum cost savings and high speed to market — 45% (2016), 63% (2015)
TCOE factory in an offshore location with high cost savings — 42% (2016), 56% (2015)

Use of direct subcontractors remains prevalent

Organizations have been locally hiring subcontractors. This is often done in emergency situations where there is no time to undertake an outsourcing exercise. Deploying subcontractors has its perils as it does not lend itself easily to:

- Knowledge retention, including knowledge hand-over when closing
- The ability to respond quickly to market dynamics
- The costs involved
- The poor economies of scale involved

Often subcontractors are independent individuals who come in for one specific project and move on to another. As such, they are not necessarily being provisioned or hired through outsourcing service providers who might be better suited to change the engagement from a staff provisioning to a managed service.

Regardless of subcontractor origins, there are shortcomings in the approach of using subcontractors. In this chapter, we will discuss the key challenges associated with facilitating subcontractors and demonstrate, through real examples, the benefits (savings) accomplished by replacing subcontractors with managed services.

It is appropriate at this point to briefly define or outline of what we mean by managed services. While there are varied definitions and service offerings, the crux is that, with managed services, the provider is responsible for ensuring the agreed upon deliverables of the engagement, regardless of the specific members working on the engagement.

Variants of managed services include risk sharing, reward and penalties, regular tracking of SLAs and KPIs, pricing for output, and many more. Needless to say, these value additions cannot be accomplished with disparate members deployed to accomplish specific tasks without a holistic view or without unified members collaborating on a shared vision.

Key challenges associated while working with subcontractors

- **Difficulty in retaining knowledge**: Subcontractors are not encouraged to document and handover knowledge. Usually, this is not even an expected **Key Performance Indicator (KPI)** for them. The current demand is for customers to work with an organization that can provide a mature and proven **knowledge management system** with world class tools. Proper documentation of knowledge has enabled organizations to create many reusable assets that will help reduce time during delivery and time to market in the future.

- **Lack of handover**: The 5-10 day notice period for releasing subcontractors does not allow for a sufficient handover of deliverables. Effective handover processes are also not employed during the handover, consequently impacting project delivery.

- **Delayed response to market dynamics**: Technology transitions in the field of Information Technology are quite common and an IT organization should be able to quickly respond to these transitions before the business is lost to competitors. Any changes to the client's IT strategy would involve change for the subcontractors too; this is generally difficult as they are usually specialists linked to a specific technology area. Organizations then must search for new subcontractors to align with their strategies, which can be time consuming, costly, and impact the *Go to Market time*.

- **Low-cost effectiveness**: Higher rates for subcontractors, compared with the internal staff or managed services cost, and combined with annual rate increases make subcontracting an expensive choice. In addition, there is the difficulty of knowledge retention, leading to an ongoing search for skills. When a new subcontract resource is identified, significant time is spent in training and grooming the resource to be productive due to a lack of handovers.
- **Poor economies of scale**: Subcontracting is often done for individual tasks and not for aggregated services, making it difficult to achieve economies of scale.

How replacing testing subcontractors with managed testing services helps

What is managed services is a topic in itself. However, for the purpose of this chapter, let's focus on how managed services resolve the aforementioned challenges about using subcontractors.

Knowledge retention

With managed services, customers benefit from an outsourcing provider with a broad talent pool of multiple skills, possessing the ability to adapt to customer-specific technology needs while providing a seamless and flexible service.

Handover

Outsource service providers have well-established notice periods with staff in the case of separations. If a staff member quits, there is a handover of responsibilities to other identified staff members to ensure project continuity.

Cost of resourcing

When there are resource changes in the team, the provider ensures both knowledge retention and handover to the new member, relieving the customer of the burden to redo the knowledge transfer.

Economies of scale

Outsource service providers offer services across multiple customers, which offer economies of scale with a large mix of skills and services. Economies of scale result in the opportunity to standardize processes, reduce duplication, and cut down the overall project spend.

As outsourcing service provider offer services across multiple customers; they also offer economies of scale across a large mix of skills and services. This continuity allows for a more standardized protocol, decreased duplication [of services], and fewer project costs.

Illustration of benefits

One of our leading banking clients with a complex and challenging project had the following challenges:

- A large contractor base led to a cost overrun as contractors were expensive
- A lack of cost-effective, skilled resources with cultural orientation

In our **Managed Testing Services (MTS)** solution, one of the transformation levers applied was *people transfer and transition*. We replaced an existing subcontractor from their workforce-testing project and deployed our career testers with cultural alignment to run the testing delivery. Our model ensured the work was carried out with a 26% productivity improvement over a 3-year period, effectively reducing the employees required to carry out the project. Using career testers, ensuring knowledge retention, accelerating automation, and leveraging our testing assets and IP were some of the techniques employed for success.

A few key highlights include:

- The client gained increased price and cost certainty, where 90% of the projects (50% BAU) were executed within the fixed price mode and bracket
- The client broke even within the first year, without any negative delivery impact
- The client received cumulative savings of 35% over three years
- Statistics showed a 26% productivity increase after three years using our MTS service

A saving calculator

The following saving calculator depicts the financial savings incurred when subcontractors working for a firm's IT delivery organization are replaced by professionals from an outsourcing services organization:

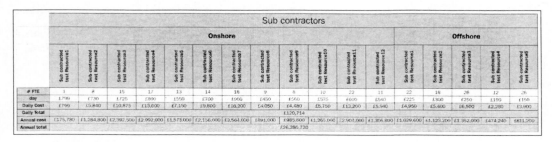

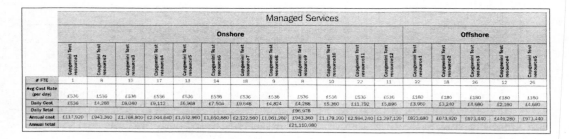

It is evident from the preceding illustration that savings of 23,738 pounds is accrued every day, resulting in a 19.7% savings/decrease on base and annual saving at 5.17 million euros. The savings are accrued through the differential cost of professionals from the outsourcing services provider relative to the direct subcontractors. The savings improve with the use of offshore locations such as India.

Conclusion

Software is now so critical to international business that it can no longer be considered a supporting or enabling technology but rather an inherent part of company strategy. Service providers must excel at understanding the subtleties of the customer's business, domain, IT ecosystem, and technology. The customer must be willing to engage with their service providers for a longer period of time and with a vision to see them as strategic partners.

Subcontracting is a tactical approach, but over-dependence on subcontractors poses some business risk, especially if the subcontractors are from smaller entities that cannot swiftly move to newer technologies. Subcontracting may still prevail for some time; however, clients must fully understand the risks involved and therefore mitigate the risks as early as possible. There should also be an attempt to maintain a ratio of subcontractors to the in-house IT staff within manageable proportions and gradually replace subcontractors with more strategic outsourcing service providers.

4

Digital Quality Assurance in a Factory Model

In this chapter, we will discuss how a *Factory* model practiced in the manufacturing world is applied in the service industry and more specifically to execute Digital Quality Assurance engagements.

In this chapter, we will discuss the following topics:

- A Digital QA Factory (DQAF) framework for industrializing Digital QA delivery
- Enablement and Service Delivery Functions of DQAF
- Benefits of using the DQAF framework

Services factories

A factory in a traditional manufacturing world visualizes a location where a set of workers performs tasks on their respective production lines.

In Services factories, developers or testers leverage a set of technologies and platforms in compliance with industrialized processes and adopt productivity-enhancing accelerators to deliver agreed outcomes.

Services factories typically offer the promise of improving the quality of service at a reduced cost and exceeding its customer's expectations. The key value levers used in a service factory include the following:

- People's skill and competencies
- Repeatable and consistent processes
- Predesigned and preconfigured tools and technologies

- Accelerated methods of carrying out tasks
- Maturing delivery models with platforms that are scalable and flexible according to client needs

A digital factory model for industrializing digital QA delivery

Testing as a Service (TaaS) model for managed testing services engagements is used by many IT service organizations. Here, we discuss a model to extend the benefits of the MTS model to quality assurance of digital initiatives in a **Digital QA Factory (DQAF)**.

A DQAF model framework is provided in schematic and is explained in the following diagram:

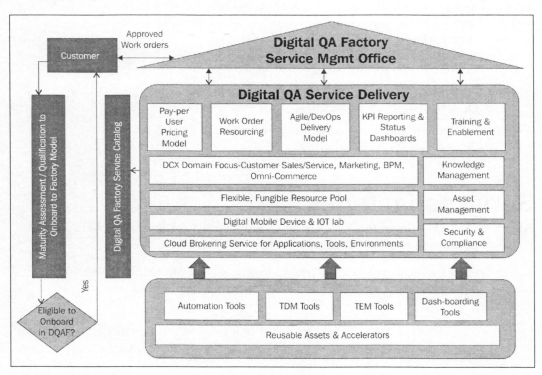

Key Elements for Onboarding in DQAF

We will now discuss the key elements presented in Digital Quality Assurance Maturity Assessment and Qualification Criteria for Onboarding in DQAF.

Key focus areas for quality assurance for the sample work packets are assessed. The assessment helps gauge the benefits to be achieved by delivering the work in DQAF. Typically, the work packets that are not repeatable in nature and cannot benefit now or in the future from reuse and automation would not be ideal candidates for DQAF.

DQAF enablement functions

The key highlights of DQAF enablement functions include the following:

- **Service Catalog**: On demand model available in addition to fixed capacity, volume and duration models. Current digital technologies demand for agility, and virtualization requires short releases. Easily accessible service catalog through an online portal enables standard services easily accessible. The KPIs/SLAs applicable for the service are also transparently listed. The service catalog lists various services, such as functional testing (ST, SIT, and E2E testing), performance testing, test automation, virtualization, and other services, along with required input, expected output, unit of measure, price per unit, and the applicable KPIs/SLAs.

- **Domain Capability and DCX focus**: DQAF acts as an integrated platform in assuring quality of delivery of digital initiatives and covers digital domains—Customer Sales or Service Management, Marketing Management, Omni-Commerce Management, and Business Process management. Adaptability, agility, and accountability in the space of **Digital Customer Experience (DCX)** Assurance of customer experience with focus on ease of use, user experience and accessibility testing is standard scope for DCX QA.

- **Customer Centric Resource Model and Governance offers following features**:
    - On-demand reporting dashboards
    - Customer-centric and optimized core resource loading
    - Fungible pool of resources to meet varied demands
    - Skill enablement and SME sourcing

Governance includes regular reporting on KPIs/SLAs and assures productivity efficiencies and predictable gains over the baseline efficiencies, based on volumes of work and service duration.

Typical SLAs tracked include the following things:

- Software Quality (defect leakage to next phase by severity)
- Time to Market (reduction in average time spent in testing)

Key Performance Indicators (KPIs) reported among others include test coverage, effort variance, and defect removal efficiency.

- **Preconfigured automation Tools, assets, and accelerators**: These reduce the lead time for implementing tools/technology and offer quick and focused validations of features and enhancements triggered due to market changes, ensuring high quality in planned or ad hoc releases. The tools can be made available in pay-for-use model over cloud. DQAF offers secure Cloud, Virtualization, Test harness and Test bed services. A dedicated mobile device/channel or an IOT lab is the key enabler for DQAF.

- **Pay-per-Use Services**: Frequent releases create a need for frequent estimates for a service. Lack of availability and access to key tools/on-demand services compounds this challenge. A pay-per-use model with service pricing predefined as per catalog addresses the challenge of frequent estimations.

DQAF service delivery functions

Digital QA service delivery function handles delivery including agile/DevOps model, work-order resourcing, and reports on SLAs/KPIs and invoices the work in pay-per-use model based on services ordered by the customer using catalog.

The DQAF service delivery function also needs to ensure asset management, knowledge management, training and enablement on training, compliance, security, and data privacy of customer assets and data.

DQAF addresses dynamicity of business processes, leverages reusable assets, offers personalized customer experience, and reduces lead time for performing QA.

Benefits delivered through DQAF model

Applying automation and reuse levers to industrialize delivery have been key cornerstones of the factory-based delivery. The concept has been extended to services, as the standard work packets of software development or test delivery can be carved out and processed in a standard manner. A digital quality assurance factory model has been discussed with key building blocks and productivity levers.

Indicative benefits delivered through DQAF include the follows:

- Improved time to market ~25%
- Reduction in production defects ~95%
- Reduced cost of QA (with improved coverage and short cycle times) ~30%
- Improved productivity through automation ~10%
- Improved automation productivity with use of standards and frameworks
- Improved productivity through reuse ~15-20%
- Predictable delivery and customer satisfaction

Conclusion

Factory model prevalent in the manufacturing world is being increasingly applied in services, specifically in software testing to bring in operating efficiencies to carry out standardized work packets in a standardized work flow. The efficiencies in DQAF model described in this chapter are achieved through implementation of various levers, such as people skills and competencies, repeatable and consistent processes, preconfigured tools, accelerators, and maturing delivery models.

We discussed the need for maturity assessment and qualification criteria for onboarding the engagements to DQAF. The key enablers for DQAF include service catalog, domain capability, resourcing model and governance with defined SLAs/ KPIs, tools and accelerators, and a pay-per-use **Testing as a Service (TaaS)** model.

We discussed delivery of Digital QA engagements through the DQAF's service delivery function.

Factory model has become popular given the benefits it offers with economies of scale of pooling the engagements. We concluded this chapter with indicative benefits achieved through the use of the model.

5

Crowdsourcing – Enabling Flexible, On-Demand Testing COEs

Crowdsourcing is leveraged in many areas. Some of the early examples of crowdsourcing include web-based dictionaries and Wikipedia. A large number of people around the world who have common interests contribute to creating something useful for the world.

Demand for crowdsourced testing is fueled by the growth in digital transformation engagements that require applications to be available across multiple channels. In this chapter, we will discuss the application of crowdsourcing in testing. We will cover the following topics:

- Trends in crowdsourced testing
- Key elements and how do they work
- Operating models
- Challenges in adoption
- Key benefits

Trends - crowdsourced testing

While a managed service model provided by an expert QA vendor ranks the highest in importance (49 %), the use of a crowdsourced solution model for quick test capacity is used by 47 % of the respondents. This puts crowdsourcing ahead of the captive **Testing Center of Excellence (TCOE)** factory (45 %), The Hybrid TCOE factory model (45 %), and a TCOE in an offshore location (42 %). This is as per the World Quality Report, 2016-17.

As cited in the latest World Quality Report, crowdsourcing offers quick, on-demand testing capabilities. Service providers are designing operating models using the hybrid TCOE (combining service provider staff in both managed service models and crowdsourced testers). This hybrid model has helped address the need for both a flexible and managed service operating model.

What is crowdtesting and how does it work?

> *"If you are testing software that all kinds of strangers are going to use, then why not use a bunch of strangers to test it?" – Paul Herzlich*

Crowdsourced testing is the process of using a tester pool to provide both formal and informal feedback on a product. Crowdtesting pilots software under real-world conditions with real users, allowing companies to gain insight and gather feedback to identify defects quickly and intelligently.

The following screenshot provides a simplified model of crowdtesting with the following key elements: crowdtesting platform, crowd, crowdtesting champion, and crowdtesting services:

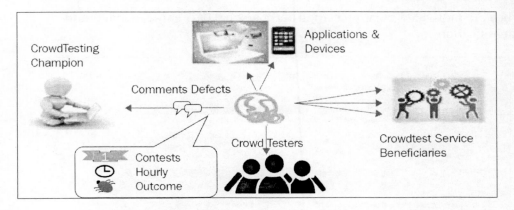

- **Crowdtesting platform**: This is a cloud-based platform. It manages testers, tracks their testing activities, curates their rankings based on the feedback given, manages compensation based on an output-based model, and integrates with standard test management tools.

- **Crowd**: This represents independent, geographically distributed testers who are part of the network and provide services upon invitation. These SMEs are willing to provide services at a precise cost and service output.

- **Crowdtesting champion**: As part of the crowdtesting management team, a champion manages deliverables by meeting client expectations. Champions could come from the customer end or be deployed from a crowdtesting service vendor.

- **Crowdtesting services**: These involve testing devices, sites, content, and other elements as requested by the customer.

Crowd can be public (for example, a subject-specific community) or private (a client workforce community or a clients' customer community). Public crowds provide global coverage on demand and on their own terms. Public crowd subjects or SMEs can be utilized for deeper analytics and identification of potential improvement. Private crowds make up part of the client workforce community with product knowledge and provide user experience. Refer to the following graph:

They are motivated by appreciation and personal or organizational brand identification.

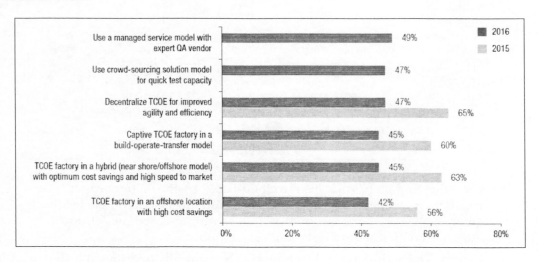

Crowdtesting operating models

There are two broad operating models prevailing for crowdsourced testing include:

- **Testing as a service**: Here, the QA vendor identifies internal employees as a private crowd along with a crowdtesting platform and testing tools to enable the client to manage end-to-end testing using their own crowdtesting champions. This is the most common format of managed crowdtesting services, and the client pays only for the outcome of the testing, for example, the number of critical bugs identified in a given time frame and the severity of the bugs.

- **On-demand tester staffing**: This is applicable when the scope of testing includes both a private and public crowd and where the client is looking to hire testers on weekly or monthly basis as retainers, instead of using an output-based model.

Crowdtesting as part of Testing Center of Excellence (TCOE)

When and where should crowdsourcing be introduced in a typical end-to-end testing engagement? Crowdtesting is often embedded in an end-to-end testing scope and employed during user acceptance testing. It is also used for niche testing needs, such as localization, translation, content testing, and accessibility testing.

Key challenges of adopting crowdtesting

Crowdsourced testing utilizes testers spread across the globe. However, typical problems with these distributed teams include the following:

- Communication challenges
- Increased management overhead
- Difficulty in obtaining stakeholder buy-in
- Problems in synchronizing all the stakeholders on product updates

Additional issues encountered in crowdsourcing include the following:

- The need to ensure the security and confidentiality of the product
- Keeping the crowd motivated and encouraged regardless of monetary returns
- Difficulty in analyzing and interpreting the varied results of a crowd's efforts
- Complexity of using multiplatform, multigeographic, and multilingual environments
- The presence of a diverse user demographic with low tolerance and a potentially negative reputation
- Concerns with quality, cost, and speed
- Issues in providing secure, dedicated access to a client network

The benefits of crowdtesting

Crowdsourced testing has many benefits, including the following:

- Native testers who use native devices for testing offer more reliable application behavior

- Crowdtesters bring the advantage of covering multiple devices, OSes, configurations, and languages

- Crowdtesters bring in knowledge of real-world scenarios for given end-user locations

- Crowdsourced testing offers a more predictable market acceptance, as the crowd acts as a beta user

- Crowds can be leveraged for user assessments across different stages of application development and serve as structured beta testing

- Crowdtesting can offer time-to-market advantages and support faster launch times

Conclusion

The world Quality Report, 2016-17, predicts that a centralized TCOE operating model will shift towards a hybrid TCOE model in order to address both flexible and managed services operating models. Crowdtesting will offer flexible, on-demand testing capabilities as part of a hybrid TCOE model. Outsourcing vendors are either partnering with crowdsourcing platform providers or developing the ability to the address crowdsourcing methodology. Digital transformation will drive the need for enterprise and disrupt the existing outsourcing models. Client will use different sourcing models to manage their testing needs while increasing costs, time-to-market, and contract duration.

References

- World Quality Report 2016-17: www.worldqualityreport.com, www.passbrains.com

- For an in-depth look at the key trends in testing and QA, download the World Quality Report, 2016, from http://ow.ly/9Ja2305zRIy

6
Testing Goes an Extra Mile over Weekends

Weekend testing is an unconventional way of testing that is influenced by a context-driven software testing philosophy. Weekend testers are typically employed professionals who come together virtually over the weekend using collaboration platforms and execute some of the most interesting software testing tasks. In a short span of time, this concept has traveled from Bangalore to the rest of the globe. Weekend testing can also be leveraged by large organizations in combination with their existing **Testing Center of Excellence (TCOE)** model. In this chapter, we will discuss the following:

- The modus operandi of weekend testing
- Advantages and disadvantages
- Trends in the use of crowdsourced testing
- How large organizations can leverage it with their TCOE model

Weekend testing – modus operandi

Weekend testing is about testers signing on to collaboration platforms, such as Skype or Google Talk, and getting started with testing at a specified time, as announced on the weekend testing website. In the group of testers, a tester assumes the role of a facilitator to bring seriousness to the mission for the session.

The bugs discovered in the course of testing are logged in a source bug database (such as Bugzilla) and followed by a debrief session. The session transcript is then posted with the results for everyone to see and analyze. The results are also shared with the client, as per the testing assignment. Weekend testing thrives on the use of open source and free tools. With so many willing, skilled, and available testers, weekend testing has become a popular forum from which testers learn, network, and earn money. With a wide variety of products to test and a myriad of testing missions to try out, there is something new to learn from every session. With people across the globe participating in these forums, we gain access to an interesting cross-section of skills and cultural trends. Although we are seeing a gradual adoption of this method, we must be wary of any risks it can bring to suppliers' reputations, such as security threats to customer knowledge assets and other operational challenges.

Advantages

Weekend testing lends itself well to areas such as localization, language, and mobile app and device testing. Its key advantages include:

- **More tester interactions and tester clubs**: Each tester builds upon their respective experiences and this collaboration enriches the quality of testing.

- **Demonstration of testing**: Questions ranging from *How can you complete testing without test cases?* and *How can you repeat testing?* to *How will the client accept that we tested?* are easily answered, thanks to a transparency policy. Testing remains open for scrutiny by anyone at any time. You can witness testing happening right in front of your eyes.

- **Tester opinion and better open source software**: Weekend testing thrives on the use of open source software for tracking bugs; as a result, clients who are averse to spending need not incur costs for purchasing commercial testing tools.

- **Scalability and time to market**: Midsized software suppliers may be forced to increase the number of team members over a limited span of time. Weekend testing can help with its vast pool of skilled and experienced testers. Moreover, as weekend testers are being spread across the globe, customers have the benefit of locating resources in their respective time zones.

- **Localization and language testing**: Weekend testing is a forum that consists of testers from various countries and cultures. Testers are readily available for localization testing and validation. Consequently, procuring a weekend tester for a specific language may be easily achieved.

- **Device and app testing**: Mobile applications need to be validated on a broad spectrum of elements that include mobile hardware, network, and OS. Software suppliers are struggling to build mobile labs that host these devices, and as such, are using emulators in the absence of devices. Weekend testing solves this logistical problem, as the tester pool is so vast. Furthermore, testing teams have a broad array of devices and OSs on which the applications may be deployed and tested. This eliminates the need to test the applications on emulators. In addition, applications are released in some regions ahead of others, and testers from these leading regions could provide the required experience to other lagging regions.

Disadvantages

While weekend testing is an interesting and evolving phenomenon, there are concerns, including the following:

- **Inadequate security**: Weekend testing does not undertake adequate measures to secure customer IPs, secure an ODC, sign NDAs, and so on, which is generally practiced by customers dealing with offshore service providers. Testing is usually done in an informal and relaxed environment; this could make clients feel skeptical about sharing their IP.

- **Inadequate alignment with business**: Weekend tester forums may not be able to swiftly respond to changes in strategy taken by customers during the project. Lack of a proper governance model and transition methodology hinders weekend testing projects from responding to changing customer needs. It may therefore pose a risk to project delivery, particularly to brand new implementations.

- **Inability to adopt DevOps**: Weekend testing relies more on open source tools and manual testing and therefore does not align well with DevOps delivery models, which promote quicker testing and integration of development test operations.

- **Governance issues**: Weekend testers often abandon tough testing sessions, leaving testing assignments incomplete for several days, thereby disrupting test continuity. Sometimes, core testers have busy weekend schedules and cannot give adequate time and commitment to their testing assignment. This greatly impacts project timelines. Lack of weekend facilitators or moderators leaves testing directionless and without any structure.

Trends in the use of crowdsourced testing

Quality is considered implicit these days. Consequently, concentration is shifting to how project testing costs can be optimized and how time to market can be improved as a measure of testing success. the World Quality Report, 2016-17, (WQR2016) cites that 42 % of IT executives want cost optimization from their respective QA functions, and 37 % of them desire faster time to market. Weekend testing can help meet these objectives and lower the cost of testing for vendors (by employing weekend testers) as well as for the customer.

Weekend testing is a form of crowdsourcing. WQR2016 has studied the use of crowdsourcing by respondents. The primary focus on achieving maximum cost efficiency in the form of operational test factory models and captive **Testing Center of Excellence (TCOE)** is moving toward a demand for more flexible, nimble, and easily accessible TCOE models, such as crowdsourcing. It is interesting to note that amid the shift, organizations still seek managed service models apart from vendors in the setup of test scenarios.

While a managed service model provided by an expert QA vendor ranks the highest in importance (49 % of respondents), the use of a crowdsourcing solution model for quick test capacity is used by 47 % of the respondents, alongside a decentralized TCOE model for improved agility and efficiency. This puts crowdsourcing ahead of a captive TCOE (45 %) and a TCOE at an offsite location (42 %).

Important elements in setting up test operations is shown in the following graph:

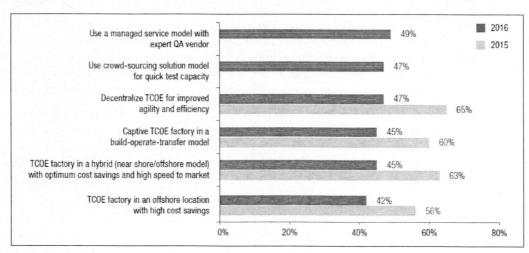

How can large IT organizations ride the weekend testing bandwagon?

Although there are few demerits of weekend testing, the power of weekend testers can still be leveraged tremendously. Some IT service providers have formed an alliance with crowd platform providers, such as Applause, as part of its Liquid Workforce Strategy. It features more than 250,000 experienced QA testers from around the world. Applause complements in-house testing professionals to provide a range of testing services and geographic coverage to their customers, especially in the areas of mobile devices, desktops, kiosks, smart TVs, wearables, and IoT testing.

A formal governance model can help integrate weekend testing teams with the test engagement teams of IT service providers. Weekend testing teams could report to meeting facilitators who typically consist of test leads or managers of test engagement. Such governance could include monitoring and reviewing of daily project activities, including weekly work schedule, progress made, and any course corrections required to meet the quality and schedule of the transition. Open issues should be highlighted and actions taken to resolve them. However, work distribution across locations, quality level, and SLA performance need to be verified. Staffing matters, such as team ramp-up and colocation, could also be discussed through formal governance.

Conclusion

Weekend testing is an interesting evolution in software testing, but its scope is currently limited to projects involving plain vanilla testing, wherein traditional models such as Waterfall and V are employed. It definitely provides advantages, such as a larger and more diverse knowledge base and increased tester experience, which lead to effective testing.

With the latest advances, such as DevOps relying heavily on automation tools, the scope for weekend testers may be limited. Weekend testing teams lack a defined structure and process and may not be able to win over the confidence of the customer. However, if a large testing organization leverages the weekend testing concept for areas such as IoT and ensures adequate governance and accountability, the concept can be employed with confidence.

References

- Capgemini, Sogeti, HPE, World Quality Report #WQR2016 (`https://www.capgemini.com/thought-leadership/world-quality-report-2016-17`)

- Website: `http://weekendtesting.com`

7

Testing in Agile Development and the State of Agile Adoption

Agile development has accelerated in the last decade due to increased digital adoption creating a need for more continuous integration. In this chapter, we will discuss Drivers for the use of Agile:

- The promise of agile as compared to waterfall
- Various flavors of agile—for example, Kanban, Scrum
- Testing in agile sprints
- Agile in distributed environments
- State of agile adoption
- Approaches to testing in agile development
- Skills needed by QA professionals in Agile engagements

A thought must be striking to you readers that *why use Agile development?*

Organizations are increasingly struggling to reach the right level of quality versus speed. Some key issues with traditional development and testing include the following:

- Excessively long time to market for products and applications
- Inadequate customer orientation and regular interaction

- Over-engineered products--most of the features on a product or application may not be used
- High project failure rate
- ROI below expectation
- Inability to respond quickly to change
- Inadequate software quality

To address this, QA and testing should be blended with agile development. Agile engagements should take a business-centric approach to select the right test focus areas, such as **behavior-driven development (BDD)**, to define acceptance criteria. This requires skills not only in testing but also in business and software development. The latest **World Quality Report** reveals an increase in the adoption of agile testing methodologies, which helps expedite time to market for products and services.

The need for agile development (and testing) is primarily driven by digital transformation. Let's take a look at the major trends in digital transformation:

- More continual integration fueled by digital transformation
- Complex integration using multi-channel, omnipresent commerce, making it necessary to integrate multiple channels, devices, and wearable technologies

Unlike yesterday's nomenclature, when agile meant colocation, today's advanced telepresence infrastructure makes it possible to work in distributed agile models and has removed any colocation dependency. Agile is not just a concept. It is a manner of working, made possible with multiple tools to enable development and testing in agile environments.

What do agile projects promise compared to traditional waterfall?

The next diagram summarizes the value an agile approach offers compared to traditional waterfall.

Waterfall engagements are characterized as plan driven. One should know the software requirements and estimate the time and effort needed to accomplish the task at hand.

In the case of agile engagements, one knows the time and resources available and needs to estimate the features that can go into a release.

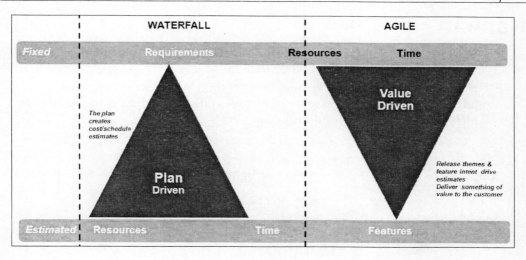

Flavors of agile

There are various flavors of agile, including the following:

- **Scrum**: This prioritizes the highest-value features and incremental delivery once every 2-4 weeks
- **Kanban**: This pinpoints bottlenecks to avoid holdups
- **Lean**: This eliminates waste and unnecessary documentation and provides future flexibility
- **XP**: This reconfigures and ensures the simplest design to deliver iteration features

Let's look at the features of each one of the preceding points.

Scrum

- Reacts quickly in volatile markets
- Focuses on customer benefits and avoids both unnecessary outlays and time investments
- Utilizes organized development teams within a structured framework in order to coordinate activities and work together for quick decision-making
- Involves customers directly in the development process

Kanban

- Works with existing roles and processes and may be introduced either step by step or by establishing pioneer teams.

- Scrum and Kanban complement one another. While Scrum ensures adaptability and agility Kanban improves efficiency and throughput. Both techniques increase overall transparency.

How is testing done in agile sprints?

I have often heard that agile projects do not require testers. Is this true? Would you compromise on quality in the name of agile?

Like any other development life cycle, agile also needs quality and testing. Agile engagements involve testers from the start of the sprint, that is, from the requirement analysis stage, in a process known as *user story grooming*.

In sprint planning, the team selects the story points depending on various factors, including availability of resources and user story complexity. All the members of the sprint team (cross-functional teams) are involved in this process (developers, business analysts, testers, configuration teams, build teams, the scrum master, and the production owner).

Once the user stories destined for the sprint are finalized, they are analyzed. Then, developers work on the design while testers write the test cases and share these with business analysts for review. At the end of each sprint, the team discloses the user stories selected during the sprint to the product owner and gets a go or no-go ruling. Once the demo is complete, the team gathers for the retrospective. Take a look at the following diagram:

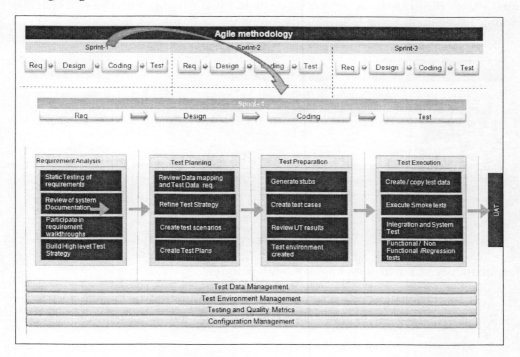

The benefits of this approach include:

- Productive, collaborative, and high-performing teams
- Predictability and project control featuring transparency and flexibility
- Superior prioritization and risk management for business success
- High-value revenue with low upfront and ongoing costs
- High-quality products delivered with minimum time to market
- Increased possibility of stakeholder engagement and high customer satisfaction

Agile in distributed environments

Often, people assume agile means colocation. Today's technology infrastructure and maturity of distributed teams have enabled agile to be practiced in a distributed mode. As per the World Quality Report 2016-2017, more than 42% of the organizations that adopt an agile delivery model use distributed agile. Distributed agile allows the organizations to achieve higher cost savings with the global delivery model. Take a look at the following diagram:

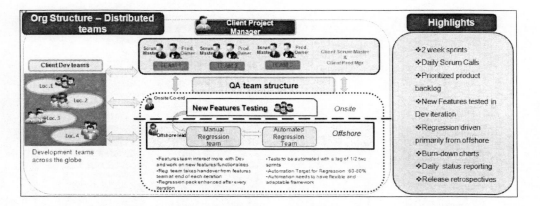

Key challenges in distributed agile model include:

- Communication challenges across the distributed team
- Increasing product backlogs
- An ever-growing regression pack
- Poor knowledge management and handover for new people due to less documentation and high-level placeholder tests
- Little time overlap with isolated regional developers for distributed teams

These challenges can be addressed through the following:

- **Communication**: Live meetings, video conference calls, and common chat rooms
- **Product backlogs**: Better prioritization within the iteration scope
- **Regression scope**: Better impact analysis and targeted regression only

- **Knowledge management**: Efficient tools and processes along with audio and video recordings of important tests, virtual scrum boards, and the latest communication and tracking tools

- **Distributed teams**: Optimal overlap timings through working shifts (40–50 %)

State of agile adoption – findings from the World Quality Report 2016-2017

As per the latest World Quality Report, there are various challenges in applying testing to agile environments. Colocation and a lack of the required skills are the two biggest challenges that are considered major risks associated with agile adoption. That said, organizations have been able to find solutions to these challenges.

Challenges in applying agile methodology

Some of the commonly known challenges in the application of agile can be seen in the following bar graph. The graph is self-explanatory:

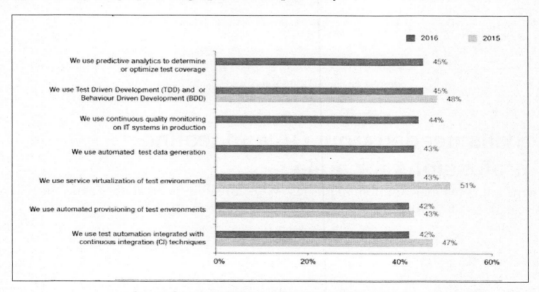

Source- Capgemini HPE Sogeti World Quality Report 2016

Approaches to testing in agile development environments

Organizations use different ways to speed up cycle times and utilize agile. Some of these tactics include predictive analytics, BDD/TDD, continuous monitoring, automated test data generation, and test environment virtualization. The following diagram provides a snapshot of the practices used to convert to agile:

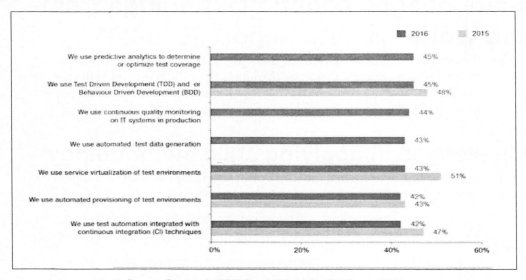

Source- Capgemini HPE Sogeti World Quality Report 2016

Skills needed from QA and testing professions for agile

The following diagram from requisites" WQR2016 depicts the state of skills relating to agile testing as organizations strive to adopt agile methodologies:

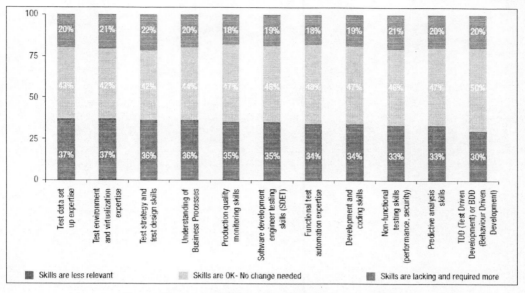

Source- Capgemini HPE Sogeti World Quality Report 2016

Conclusion

An ideal agile engagement needs a test ecosystem that is flexible and supports both continual testing and quality monitoring. Given the complexity in agile engagements, automated decision-making to achieve both speed and quality would be invaluable.

Agile development has attained critical mass and is now being widely adopted; the initial hesitation no longer prevails. The QA function is a key enabler in this journey. The coexistence of traditional IT along with agile delivery principles is giving rise to a new methodology based on bimodal development.

8

Agile and DevOps Adoption are Gaining Momentum

In the previous chapter, we discussed testing in agile development and the state of agile adoption. In this chapter, we will discuss key trends relating to the increased adoption of agile development:

- Increased use of agile/DevOps principles
- Increased complexity of testing in agile engagements
- Challenges in setting up agile **Testing Center of Excellence (TCOE)**
- Readiness of the QA discipline to meet the demands of agile/DevOps engagements
- Difference in testing DevOps with regard to traditional engagements

Increased adoption of agile methodologies and DevOps is helping businesses roll out new products and services at greater speed.

Findings from WQR 2016 indicate increased maturity with better appreciation of the true purpose and application of DevOps. 42 % of the respondents reported an uptick in continuous monitoring with predictive analysis along with an increased use of cloud-based environments.

Colocation and the lack of the required skill sets are the two biggest risks associated with agile and DevOps adoption. However, organizations are able to find solutions to these challenges in order to increase the implementation of agile methodologies. 44 % of businesses are reluctant to include testing teams in the initial planning phase, as they believe it would inhibit release speed and risk business security.

Success stories in distributed agile methodology are enabling faster proliferation of agile principles. WQR 2016 indicates over 42 % of the organizations that adopted the agile delivery model currently use distributed agile methodologies. These methodologies allow an organization to achieve higher cost savings associated with the global delivery model. From a skill set perspective, the supply and demand gap is also narrowing and more than 80 per cent of project managers believe that they have the right skill sets needed for agile and DevOps delivery.

Increased use of agile/DevOps principles

As per WQR 2016, over 40 % of the participants cite that more than 50 % of the projects use agile/DevOps principles. The percentage of those not using agile/DevOps has dropped from 18 per cent in 2015 to 12 % in 2016.

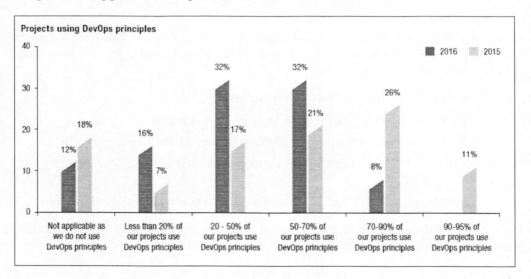

Increased complexity of testing in the agile landscape

The report finds that DevOps implementation challenges go far beyond issues with QA, and businesses risk isolating the benefits of DevOps if they are unable to break down business silos. DevOps and agile delivery methodologies are gaining wide acceptance at a rapid pace. More and more organizations are adopting new ways of delivering IT projects, based on agile principles.

With the advent of mobile, digital, and cloud-based technologies, the IT landscape is changing fast. There is continuous demand from the business to deliver new and improved IT solutions to end users. Time to market is shrinking and application complexity is increasing. At the same time, quality expectations are rising. For applications, especially those based on clouds, a higher level of testing is needed to ensure performance and security requirements are met. Testing complexity is enhanced further due to multiple access channels and various mobile and handheld devices that need to be supported by modern-day digital applications.

Identifying the right focus areas for testing and involving testing teams early, right from planning and inception stages, are considered the top two challenges for agile implementation. This creates difficulty with regard to allocating the appropriate level of test types and test depth to meet project requirements.

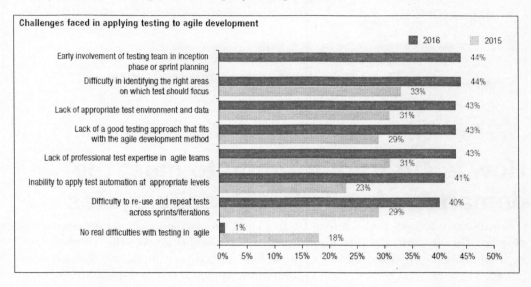

Challenges cited in setting up agile test COEs

While there has been an increase in the use of agile/DevOps life cycles, there has been an increase in challenges cited as well. The top three challenges in setting up an agile Test COE, as cited by participants, include the following:

- Necessity to colocate the team that denies cost savings

- Independent test vendors' unwillingness to pair up testers with developers
- Agile being used as an excuse to not have documentation

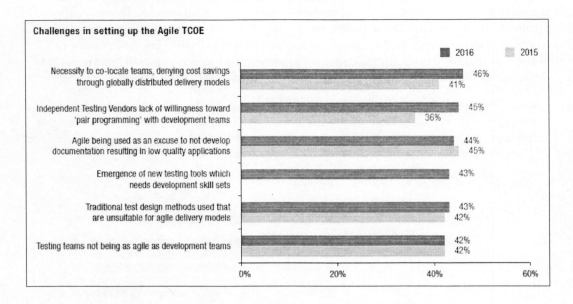

How is QA transforming to meet the demands of agile/DevOps life cycles

It is important to note that while agile and DevOps practices strive for faster software delivery, quality, and stability, security of applications is always the first priority in any business. Any failure of IT applications has a direct impact on the corporate image. The aim of a QA is to develop the internal capability to deliver software faster to support the needs of the business; however, the software must also satisfy the needs of the end user. This is achieved by developing an environment where an application can be tested early, optimally, and quickly. It is also equally important to be able to monitor quality continuously in production and test environments.

In order to maximize the effectiveness of the QA function, organizations should ensure that the basic principles of agile (that is, to communicate, collaborate, and integrate) are practiced in a continuous and consistent manner. Additionally, QA teams should become an integral part of the technical team. This helps QA to actually become facilitators of quality.

Organizations also need to define the desired level of quality. Instead of reaching for perfection in software, the focus should instead be on a *satisfying user experience within the given resources and the given time frame*. Testers should choose metrics that bring to light software defects early in the life cycle. They should also adopt lean and agile principles to develop software in small increments. The focus should be on automated regression testing for high-risk areas, using risk-based testing. Automation should be leveraged to the maximum extent.

Behavior Driven Development (BDD) is fast gaining popularity as it is a customer-centric testing methodology that implements an acceptance-criteria-based test strategy. Zero touch test automation is the ultimate goal of a QA in order to meet time-to-market objectives while maintaining test coverage.

What is the difference between testing in DevOps and traditional life cycle?

While traditional testing places a very high emphasis on process standardization and optimization, DevOps QA focuses more on agility and time to market. Skill sets needed for QA professionals are also undergoing a considerable change. Today's testers adopt continuous testing techniques, leverage automation, and deploy emerging technologies, such as cloud-based environments and service virtualization.

The mindset of a QA in DevOps is very different from that of a QA in an organization 10 years ago. In the past, the primary job of a tester was to find bugs. Today, QA groups are charged with the responsibility of preventing defects from reaching the end user. QA takes on a critical role in DevOps because it has the visibility and the directive to push code out when it is working and roll it back when it is not.

The skill set required for a QA engineer requires a fine mix of technical and business skills. Testers are quality advocates, influencing both development and operational processes. They don't just find bugs. They look for any opportunity to improve repeatability and predictability.

QA owns the process of continuous improvement and quality tracking across the entire development life cycle. Testers should have a thorough knowledge of application architecture and design. They should be able to participate in design- and architecture-based discussions and check for product scalability. They should create high quality and maintainable automation frameworks. They should also be capable of building, deploying, managing, and customizing their own test environments and test data.

Conclusion

Agile development has now attained critical mass and is being widely adopted. The initial hesitation does not prevail anymore. The QA function is a key enabler in this journey. The use of predictive analytics to determine and optimize test coverage alongside the usage of BDD techniques provides the perfect combination of shift left and shift right techniques. The coexistence of traditional IT along with agile delivery principles is giving rise to a new methodology based on bimodal development.

9

Does the Rise of DevOps Undermine Agile?

The question may come to you; can agile survive as DevOps becomes more ubiquitous? agile methods in software development have been practiced over the last two decades. The last 4-5 years have, in addition, seen the rise of DevOps methods. There have been questions on whether DevOps replaces agile. Agile is a philosophy that found acceptance as being against the waterfall model, as organizations increasingly struggled to match the right level of quality versus speed. While agile is often a way of thinking prevalent in anything that a company does with speed, here we limit ourselves to the uses of **agile** in IT.

In this chapter, we will cover the following topics:

- Agile, DevOps, and the respective drivers for the use of each
- Agile is about speed and DevOps removes boundaries between development, QA, and operations
- Compare and contrast agile and DevOps

We will conclude the debate with the fact that agile and DevOps complement each other and are not substitutes.

Agile is about speed

The drivers for the increased use of agile include:

- Excessively long time-to-market for products and applications
- Inadequate customer orientation and regular interaction
- Over-engineered products—most of the features on a product or application may not be used
- High project failure rate
- ROI below expectations
- Inability to respond quickly to change
- Inadequate software quality

The key digital trends that have caused an increased use of agile include:

- More continuous integration fueled by digital transformation
- Complex integration using multichannel and omnipresent commerce, making it necessary to integrate multiple channels, devices, and wearable technology

In agile engagements, one knows the time and resources available and needs to estimate the features that can go into a release. Two popular modes of agile include:

- Scrum (prioritizes the highest value features and incremental delivery once every 2-4 weeks)
- Kanban (pinpoints bottlenecks to avoid hold-ups)

Agile engagements follow sprints and in each sprint (requirement, design, code, test) planning, the team selects the story points depending on various factors, including the availability of resources and user story complexity. All the members of the sprint team (cross-functional teams) are involved in this process (developers, business analysts, testers, configuration teams, build teams, the scrum master, and the production owner).

Once the user stories destined for the sprint are finalized, they are analyzed. Then, the developers work on the design while the testers write test cases and share these with business analysts for review. At the end of each sprint, the team discloses the user stories selected during the sprint to the product owner and gets a go or no go ruling. Once the demo is complete, the team gathers for the retrospective. Initially, agile meant co-location; today's advanced tele-presence infrastructure makes it possible to work in distributed agile models and has removed the co-location dependency.

Chapter 9

DevOps removes the boundaries between dev, QA, and operations

This ultimately leads to an IT process with a continuous stream of IT updates to the end user. DevOps is all about delivering technology to business in an uninterrupted and non-disruptive fashion. DevOps focuses on automated deployment processes and a high level of communication between operations and software development teams.

As per WQR 2016, there are various challenges in applying testing to agile/DevOps environments. Co-location and a lack of required skills are the two biggest challenges that are considered major risks associated with agile/DevOps adoption. That said, organizations have been able to find solutions to these challenges. Organizations use different ways to speed up cycle times and utilize agile. Some of these tactics include predictive analytics, BDD/TDD, continuous monitoring, automated test data generation, and test environment virtualization.

Agile versus DevOps

Agile is all about cycle-time reduction in multiple ways: shrink the entire development life cycle, automate various stages, and more. Agile focuses more on individuals and interactions than on the processes and documentation relevant to traditional development. DevOps, by nature, would have multiple teams which can be practicing various agile/non-agile principles to deliver continuous development, continuous integration, continuous testing, and continuous deployment with a high focus on leveraging automation:

	Agile	DevOps
Values	Agile manifesto and agile principles	Focus on service and value being delivered to the end-user
Target Areas	Software Development	End-to-end solution delivery
Methods	Scrum, Kanban, XP,..	Extended implementation of agile methods entire value chain integrated into one system.
Practices	Tactical techniques	Continuous integration and deployment, tool change, virtualization, and other techniques to accelerate change and lower the risk.
Shift-Left Principles	Leverages Shift-Left	Leverages both Shift-left and Shift-Right
Tools	Jira, Bugzila, Kanboard, etc	Puppet, CHEF, Teamcity, Openstack, AWS

Conclusion

Agile and DevOps are not substitutes.

DevOps leverages agile's **Definition of Done** within the CI/CD framework.

While ideally DevOps engagements should follow agile methods, even Waterfall or Iterative models can leverage DevOps by integrating Dev-Test-Ops. Hence, it is not appropriate to think that agile is contained within DevOps or is a sub-set of DevOps. Both stand on their own, independently.

To conclude, agile and DevOps co-exist and complement each other.

10

Role of Automation in DevOps Life Cycle

Today's IT industry is embracing scenarios where the continuously churned out code can be built and deployed within minutes and even seconds. Deploying code changes from the source-code repository at defined and set time-intervals is a thing of past. In addition to the pace of deployment, there is also a need to validate and ensure that high quality of code is maintained for end user satisfaction. The challenge for the software development teams, thus, becomes the alignment of velocity and quality. Here, velocity is the speed at which the software is being developed according to the requirements and quality is to ensure that standards are being adhered to. Is there a way that the quality goals are verified and satisfied as soon as the software gets deployed?

Many organizations are transitioning to agile and DevOps practices that will enable them to bridge this gap between code deployment and quality validation and signoff.

In this chapter, we will discuss:

- The importance of automation in DevOps
- Automating during early integration
- Automation as a by default practice
- Deployment automation
- Automation – metrics and measures
- Best practices for early adoption and continuous automation

The importance of automation in DevOps

The foundation of DevOps incorporates built-in automation in the software development life cycle from as early as the requirements phase till the fag end of operations:

- Manual static testing of requirements is now being replaced by **Acceptance Test-Driven Development (ATDD)** and/or **Behavior-Driven Development (BDD)**

- ATDD and BDD using Cucumber, Fitnesse or RSpec help in documenting requirements, while also automating them

- This automation is accomplished by **Software Development Engineers in Testing (SDETs)**, who possess both development and testing skills

- While BDD is taking place, the development team can use xUnit tools such as NUnit or JUnit to work on the **Test-Driven Development (TDD)**

- All these tests can be integrated with the **Continuous Integration (CI)** server in order to initiate test execution along with build creation in the pre-deployment phase

Such techniques bring in the *Shift Left* approach to quality where a thorough requirements testing and unit testing takes place.

This will not change the fact that requirements may still continue to change throughout the development cycle and that these changes will need to go through a similar automation cycle.

However, it surely takes care of one thing, and that is the existing requirements are well understood by the development and the test teams, bringing the entire team on the same page.

Early integration automation

Since partial automation has already taken place as part of BDD and TDD, and is integrated with the CI server, the service level components can be targeted next as the **User Interface (UI)** is yet to be made available.

Also, there are times when basic UI automation can be accomplished using mocks and stubs. However, the scripts undergo changes once the final UI is ready. The effort to modify the existing scripts is directly proportional to the quality of mocks and stubs that were provided during the initial automation work.

To enable integration, the CI server builds the system on demand, on schedule, or even as soon as the code is checked in.

- Each developer can run and test the code on his/her system to ensure that the code is not broken
- For an early and extensive integration testing, the test team can utilize the features of service, application, and network virtualization

Whether it is UI integration with service a or database layer, or it is the integration of one system with other systems and utilities, virtualization provides solutions in many ways, focusing on the *shift-left* approach for testing and the ability to run end-to-end scenarios. The service virtualization tools such as CA LISA, IBM Rational Integration Tester, HP Service Virtualization, and Parasoft Virtualize, help with the following:

- Shortening the release cycle
- Identifying bugs early in the software life cycle

Since the availability of dedicated test environments at an earlier stage of software lifecycle is rare, virtual test environments or server virtualization can be used to create an environment to run service-level tests and other automated scripts. Refer to the following diagram:

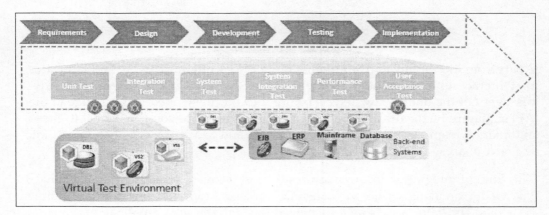

The interacting and dependent systems' behavior, data, and performance characteristics can be captured and simulated using service virtualization.

The captured services and simulated test data can be deployed on the test environment to represent the dependent system for a seamless early integration test to occur. Take a look at the following diagram:

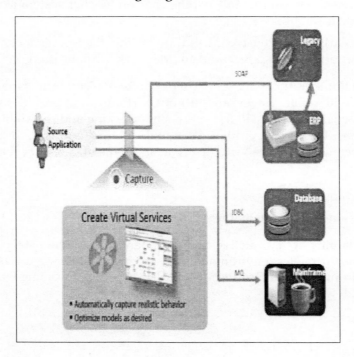

Apart from identifying and simulating the services, automating the API interfaces that interact with each other by understanding the API signature allows the early discovery of the underlying defects before the UI is developed. Any change in the API signature by the development team should ideally be communicated to the automation team for a timely update of scripts and to avoid leakage of defects into the next phases.

This kind of integration testing requires the test teams to possess enough technical knowledge on using service virtualization tools and to write API/interface testing code bits. The value and benefits achieved through service virtualization the following:

- Faster time to market
- Reduced number of defects
- Continuous availability of services

Automation – the default practice

Making automation a default and implicit practice in an agile and DevOps environment helps in ensuring the following:

- The existing functionality, if broken by any new code check-in, is called out and reported immediately

- The developer is notified and is required to fix it as it happens

- The coverage of testing grows as the existing functionality gets validated by automated scripts on daily and nightly builds

- The test team can focus on validating new functionality, thus, increasing the velocity of development

While TDD, ATDD, BDD, and service virtualization, all focus on the inside-out view of testing, the test-after approach calls for parallel independent testing that looks at the outside-in aspect of the software.

To ensure that the pace and quality of agile development and testing is maintained in a DevOps implementation framework, refer to the following points:

- Automated execution of a minimal set of features in every testable build is advised

- The functionality of the system can be automated using tools such as Selenium, HP Unified Functional Tester, Eggplant, and more

- The order and priority of features to be automated, when aligned with the iteration and the release plan, will ensure high returns on investment

For instance, if the User Registration Form feature is required to proceed to perform further actions in an application, it would be advisable to automate the feature, include positive and negative scenarios, and execute them on all the released builds. This would ensure that the existing feature is not broken and is tested through automation, and thus, the test team can continue to test the rest of the released and dependent features. This induces confidence about the quality of the software/ application under development.

A continuous practice of building executable automation code for prioritized features along with the APIs and services test code and integrating this automated code with the CI server saves time on deployment and execution and, therefore, provides high ROI and reduced time to market. Take a look at the following diagram:

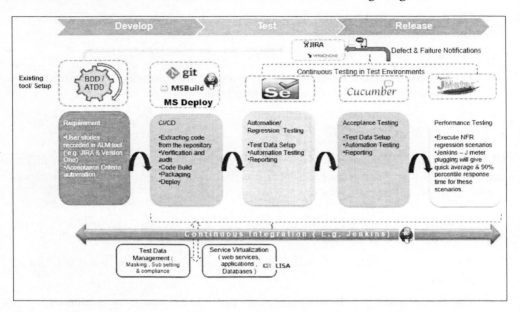

Deployment automation

Continuous development, continuous integration of the code, and continuous deployment onto physical, virtual, and cloud environments enable continuous testing. If the regression, services, security, and performance test suites are integrated with the continuous server, they can be triggered as soon as the build is deployed on the target environment. Creating an automation suite for UAT scenarios and specific production scenarios help in performing the pre- and post-deployment tests and shorten the feedback cycles.

Automation – metrics and measurements

Often, when the automation is carried out only after the entire product is ready, the number of times the automation execution is carried out is restricted due to the lack of time. On adding the development and maintenance effort to this, the returns on the investment in automation drastically reduce and sometimes move to negative.

To make an effective investment, it is critical to start automation early on for the prioritized features, based on the release schedule.

A regular tracking and monitoring system will accentuate the measurements and course corrections as required. Some of the key metrics to track are automation coverage, automation index, framework and scripts reusability, automation scripting and execution productivity, and automation ROI.

Automation coverage

This is usually measured as the number of automatable test cases out of the total number of test cases in the Regression and Functional test suite. An average of 70%-80% coverage can be achieved by automating the functionality, regression, and service-level automation. Bringing in the end-to-end interface automation can increase the coverage percentage.

Automation index

The number of automated scripts executed out of the total number of test cases that are selected for the given Test Cycle, gives the Automation Index. The higher the index, the higher is the ROI, and the benefits of automation.

Framework and scripts reusability

Having a robust and extensible automation framework makes automation adoption easy and a viable option. It is also key that the framework follows modular programming practices, allowing the reuse of scripts and module libraries. This metric can be measured after initial adoption is completed.

Automation scripting and execution productivity

The number of scripts that can be produced and executed in a given time period, say, a day, shows the team's productivity. This productivity number when compared to the manual productivity, should result in a huge reduction of effort to consider the automation project successful. This productivity data usually shows improvement over time when folded in with the reusability factor as well as increased domain and application knowledge in the team.

Automation ROI

The total effort spent on automation includes time for the following:

- Framework design
- Script creation
- Reviews and testing
- Maintenance effort over releases to incorporate release-specific changes
- The time taken to execute test cases in each test cycle

Comparing this time with manual effort for test execution shows the ROI. If, in spite of having automation scripts, the test cases are still being executed manually, the ROI on automation would be considered negative.

Another aspect to keep in purview while calculating the ROI is the time spent on analyzing failed scripts. Some scripts fail due to the issues or defects in the application and analyzing them does not take much effort. If the scripts fail due to any other reason, such as errors in script logic, network latency, third-party utility connectivity delays, and so on., and if the time taken to analyze such errors is longer, it has a direct and adverse impact on the productivity and ROI.

Automation progress tracking

Since automation work is considered as a separate unit of work, it is important that a project schedule is maintained and tracked closely. Daily, weekly, and monthly status reports should have a section to report the automation metrics as discussed in the preceding section, risks and dependencies, and so on. in order to ensure the obstacles are cleared on time.

Best practices to adopt early and continuously automate

Like any other practice, automation requires some basic tenets to be in place for it to be successful. Some of them are as follows:

- Treating automation as any other development work
- Quality engineering
- Coupling of development, automation, and test teams
- Selecting the right solution

Treating automation as any other development work

Since automation becomes the engine to run DevOps seamlessly, it is critical to maintain a similar discipline. Automation should be treated as any other development work. Starting with the framework design to coding standards, to code reviews and unit testing of the code/scripts, the team should be aligned and should sign up to follow the best practices, whatsoever. Any new work would easily mold itself into the implementation framework, reducing the ramping up and initiation efforts. This will have a direct and positive impact on the ROI.

Quality engineering

Start automation as early as possible, thus moving the focus from mere testing to quality engineering. Practices such as BDD, service testing, API testing, and performance engineering bring out the engineering aspect of testing and help find and fix defects much earlier in the cycle.

Coupling of development, automation, and test teams

If a physical co-location of the development and test teams is not possible, a virtual coupling using centralized tools, daily standup meetings, and regular interactions is key to synchronize the teams together. Having the builds deployed on the test environment either on cloud or virtual systems is required to continuously execute automated scripts and provide regular feedback.

Selecting the right solution

There are multitude of solutions available on the market for automation adoption. Some tools focus only on one aspect, such as JUnit for TDD or Selenium for functional testing. The end-to-end automation solutions where most of these tools are integrated centrally using custom code with a continuous integration server, say Jenkins or Bamboo, for a seamless implementation are usually owned by organizations themselves or by some key vendors, such as HP, and so on.

Choosing the right automation approach and solution is key to the successful and smooth functioning of DevOps implementation.

Conclusion

Automation is an important activity in the DevOps life cycle. Automation can bring results in DevOps if practiced early. In this chapter, we discussed *Early integration* and automating by default. Automation should focus on all activities—design/build and deploy. Metrics to track automation have been discussed. Best practices in early adoption and continuous automation have been presented.

11

Assessing the State of Your DevOps Adoption with DevOps Benchmarking Approach

Previously on DevOps, we discussed *New Breed of Testers with DevOps (Reference -1)*. We discussed the evolution of DevOps, DevOps approach, use of tools in DevOps life cycle, and how DevOps has changed the skill landscape expected of test organizations. In this chapter, we will discuss how an organization should go about assessing the state of readiness for DevOps and mature in their DevOps journey.

To begin with, let's discuss briefly why organizations are moving to DevOps and any challenges in doing so. Then I will present a method to assess the current state of maturity and a roadmap to achieve a higher state of maturity in the DevOps journey.

Why DevOps – the drivers

DevOps speeds up IT to achieve business agility. Compared with traditional IT, DevOps does the following:

- Redefining teams to eliminate silos and barriers to progress (traditional silos being Business/Dev/QA/Ops)

- Restructuring the approach to Release Planning—favoring small rapid releases to production over large groups of changes

- Adopting agile and lean concepts across the entire end-to-end life cycle

DevOps maximizes automation across build, testing, provisioning, configuration management, promotion, deployment, and release stages.

Challenges organizations face in implementing DevOps

So we agree, there is business case for DevOps adaption, and it provides the required agility to businesses in today's fast-paced business environment. Is it easy then for an organization to implement DevOps? We need to know the challenges and be prepared. As per WQR2016, some of the challenges (the percentages of respondents citing the challenge are in parentheses) in adapting DevOps include:

- Insufficient speed in testing due to insufficient levels of test automation (39%)

- Difficulty in identifying the right areas on which the test should focus (33%)

- Lack of appropriate test environments and data (31%)

- Lack of professional test and quality expertise in teams (31%)

- Lack of good testing approach that fits with the DevOps approach (29%)

- Difficulty to reuse and repeat tests across iterations (29%)

DevOps QA benchmarking — why and what?

To understand the current state of maturity of the organization to adapt to DevOps practices is important in ensuring successful implementation of DevOps. A baseline assessment helps to understand the challenges (such as those stated in the preceding section) to be acknowledged and addressed before an organization can embark on the DevOps journey, for those who have already embarked on the journey, such assessment helps to progress further in achieving a higher state of DevOps maturity.

The DevOps QA benchmarking framework assesses the maturity of the testing processes in a DevOps environment and helps us to develop a roadmap for envisioned end state.

Key DevOps practices (as against traditional IT) include the following:

- Use of an integrated Quality approach
- Build quality engineering teams in DevOps
- Implement Behavior-Driven and Test-Driven Development
- Automate, Automate, Automate, to enable a Zero-touch continuous automated testing
- Virtualize test environment, and automate test data needs for continuous integration
- Implement quality metrics for DevOps
- Continuously monitor quality of **Continuous Integration/Continuous Deployment (CI/CD)**

Benchmarking of the 25 elements of DevOps QA across 6 areas — source control, build management, release management, deployment, test management, and monitoring is done as follows.

The 4 states in the level of maturity for DevOps benchmarking include the following:

- **Initial**: This involves agile development, limited automation, focus on code quality, and versioning traditional infrastructure

- **Controlled**: This involves continuous integration, automated build, QA Integration simulation, business process modeling, and continuous testing

- **Efficient**: This involves extended testing automation, process optimization, analytics, automated Provisioning, and cloud Lite

- **Optimizing**: This involves process productization, managed KPI trajectory, and hybrid cloud

DevOps QA benchmarking assessment areas

With this proposed toolkit for DevOps QA benchmarking assessment, we assess the current state of each of the practices in the 25 elements in the 6 key areas on a scale of 1-4.

The 6 areas of assessment with overall 25 elements assessed for the state of maturity on a scale of 1-4 are listed here:

Source Control:

- Software Configuration Management
- Frequency of Code Commits
- Unit Testing
- Branching Complexity
- Infrastructure Version Control

Build Management:

- Build Infrastructure
- Automated Build Management
- Build Repository
- Dependencies Management
- Cluster Management
- Virtual Machine Management
- Gated Commits

Test Management:

- Test Process Management
- Continuous Automation
- Non-Functional Testing
- Service Virtualization
- Test Data Automation

Deployment:

- Automated Deployment
- Notifications
- Database Configuration

Release Management:

- Release Process
- Roll-Back Process

Monitoring:

- Continuous Monitoring
- Metrics Analysis
- Dashboard and Reporting

Outcome of DevOps QA benchmarking assessment

A sample snapshot of the DevOps QA Benchmarking assessment is provided in the following graph:

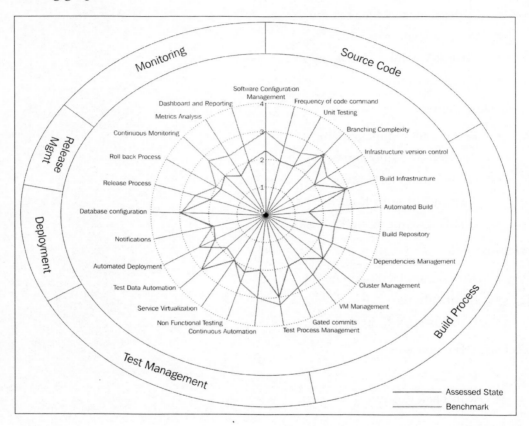

Conclusion

The organizations practicing DevOps should have a benchmark database of DevOps maturity across engagements and domains. Engagement assessments should be carried out for respective engagements and should be compared against benchmarks, as portrayed in the preceding kiviatt chart. The assessment helps identify areas of gaps, based on which actions can be identified for advancing in the DevOps maturity roadmap for the envisioned end state.

12
Accelerating DevOps – ChatOps is the New Cool

In a relationship, communication is the most important thing – Anonymous.

Communication is cited as the most important aspect in any relationship and in the success of any initiatives. Success of IT projects depends on the robust communication process. With emergence of social media, chats have become a well-accepted means of communication when it comes to approaching an IT help desk, resolving tickets, and so on.

In the context of the increased use of DevOps, communication becomes even more important as DevOps covers the entire life cycle from software development to IT operations. In this chapter, we will discuss ChatOps, that has emerged as one of the most efficient tools in effectively implementing DevOps.

DevOps trends from World Quality Report

Organizations are adopting Agile and DevOps at a very fast pace. As we discussed in Chapter 7, *Testing in Agile Development and the State of Agile Adoption* ,and Chapter 8, *Agile and DevOps Adoption are Gaining Momentum,* as per WQR2016, only 12% of CIO respondents said that they were not using DevOps in their projects. Refer to the following graph:

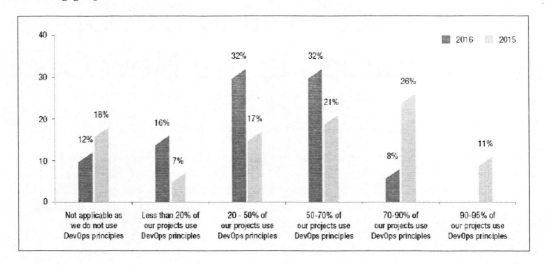

Projects using DevOps principles

The WQR2016 report also talks about new approaches to increase the quality of DevOps, which includes leveraging predictive analytics, using a cloud based testing environment with virtualization, combining shift-left and shift-right, and focusing on the mixed skill set of DevOps and Agile development. From the past few years, ChatOps is also emerging as one of the promising accelerators for DevOps. ChatOps—Background and Need.

In past the few years, DevOps has evolved at a very fast pace and the whole IT industry is confidently banking on it as it provides a unique combination of people, process, tools, and automation. Continuous integration, continuous deployment, and continuous testing have become the new mantras.

Recently, ChatOps has emerged as one of the most effective techniques to implement DevOps. It accelerates the DevOps culture, which provides better collaboration among people and automation through bots, which finally results in greater efficiencies. Take a look at the following screenshot:

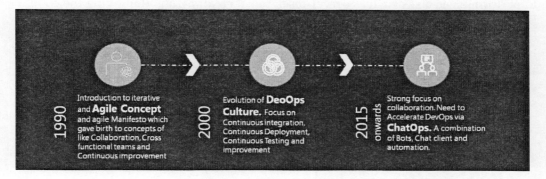

The spirit of DevOps lies in **culture of automation, measurement, and sharing (CAMS)**. ChatOps focuses on the CAMS spirit through automation of common and repeatable tasks, effective collaboration among different teams, and distribution of real-time information. The benefits are in terms of shortening the feedback loop and lowering the response time. Through ChatOps, we can do many things such as deploying code from Chat, viewing graphs from a logging tool, or creating new Jira tickets.

ChatOps – How does it work?

The basic structure of ChatOps and mapping of testing steps is provided in the following screenshot:

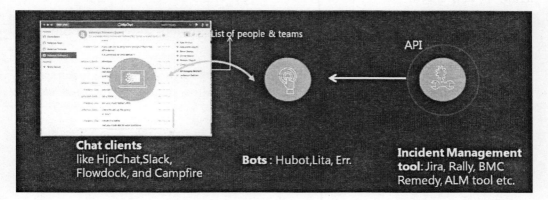

In the DevOps environment, teams use chat clients such as HipChat, Slak, or Flowdock for their regular communication. This is integrated with bots such as Hubot, Lita, or Err. A chat client manages a group of people who are responsible to address issues and incidents. A user can give commands to bots via a chat window to perform basic tasks such as server reset, ticket creation, and deploying the code. Bots in the background are connected with an API of any incident management or the **Application Life cycle Management (ALM)** tool from where they fetch the required information. When an issue is generated, everyone who is a part of the chat knows it. This helps to identify the correct person to resolve the issue. ChatOps as a concept can be applied to various types of services such as application management services, and testing services.

Application of ChatOps as a collaboration platform

In application maintenance services, ticket handling teams are organized from L1 to L4 based on the skills required for ticket resolution. When there is an application outage, a ticket flows from L1 to L4, but there is always an ambiguity in terms of a single point of ownership. *Who is the ticket escalated to* is a major challenge for the earlier lines of defense. A ChatOps approach works well here, where a ticket is escalated to a group of people having a different type of skill sets and experiences. Anyone who identifies the problem can take ownership and solve it immediately. Integrated bots allow teams to perform some automated tasks trough commands.

Early involvement of the testing team has always been a challenge for projects. There are many situations, from requirement gathering to implementation of code and finally test. A group of cross-skilled testers in collaboration with the development team can help identify defects early. ChatOps provides that collaboration platform where testers and developers can experience the true DevOps culture and its bots feature works as an accelerator. Tasks such as deployment of code and running test scripts, can be executed through a chat window.

This type of conversion-driven development provides IT professionals, testers, engineers, and customers a better approach to communicate among themselves.

Benefits of ChatOps

The concept of ChatOps provides several benefits:

- **Everybody is aligned on an issue**: It is difficult to manage a large volume of e-mails and track it until they are resolved.

- **Improved time to resolution**: Agility of cross-functional teams improves through communication and deployment of bots for automated tasks, resulting in a lower resolution time.

- **Offers virtual organizations without the need for changing organization structures**: Through ChatOps, we can virtually combine skilled people from various fields into a team regardless of their location.

- **Automation**: One of the most important achievement is the integration of bots. They are our helpers who perform tasks as directed via programmed commands. This dramatically decreases time spent on an issue because functions such as content search, code deployment, and server reset can be easily assigned to bots.

Conclusion

Based on the WQR2016, DevOps is implemented by organizations in 20%-70% of their projects and has become a necessity for almost every organization. Customers want time-to-market and issue resolution times to be as low as possible. ChatOps is a means for vendors to accelerate their projects and provide better efficiencies to customers.

13
Behavior-Driven Development (BDD) Using Gherkin in Agile/DevOps Environment

In the earlier chapters, we discussed the growing adoption of Agile/DevOps and the need for testers to be skilled in scripting language to be able to test in DevOps projects. DevOps engagements use the **Behavior-Driven Development (BDD)** approach, where cross-functional teams explore the product for features to be develop and behaviors required in software application/product. Luckily, scripting for DevOps engagements is made easy with use of English-like scripting tools.

In this chapter, we will discuss the basics of the Gherkin language, roles in a DevOps team using the BDD approach, and benefits of using the Gherkin language.

Background – Behavior-Driven Development (BDD)

In the Agile/DevOps environment, the features of the product/application being developed are co-engineered by business analysts, vendors, development, and the testing team. Given the engagement structure where various technical and non-technical members work together, a plain English construct for scripts comes in handy. Such constructs have little structure, and are very easy to learn even by non-programmers, yet structured enough to allow precise description of test examples to show business flows.

One such language using plain English construct is Gherkin. One can develop the tests using Gherkin languages and create a `.feature` file containing the executable specifications for the behaviors expected. Then a tool like *Cucumber* can be used to execute/test the features.

In this section, we will touch upon a plain English-like construct of the *Gherkin* language for BDD in the Agile/DevOps environment and discuss various activities and roles involved in performing BDD using Gherkin and benefits of using the BDD framework with Gherkin.

Gherkin – basic syntax and illustration

Gherkin uses a declarative textual format for the features to be tested. It has a line-oriented approach as a language and uses indentation for defining structure. Each source file of Gherkin consists of only one feature description. Let's discuss the syntax used in Gherkin Language:

- **Feature**: This is a brief description of what is desired as part of the business flow / use cases. It provides the business rules that govern the scope of the feature and any additional information that will make the feature easier to understand.
- **Scenario**: This is some determinable business flow.
- **Given**: This is some precondition.
- **And**: This is some other precondition.
- **When**: This is some action by the actor.
- **And**: This is some other action.
- **And**: This is yet another action.
- **Then**: This is some testable outcome achieved.

Also, something else we can check happens too:

Scenario: This is a different flow.

In the preceding Gherkin syntax:

- **Feature**: This describes the business flow of the feature to be verified
- **Scenario**: This is from where the scenario steps to be verified starts from
- **Given**: This is used to provide the system a present state before the scenario is executed
- **When**: This describes what action a user will perform

- **Then**: This is the resultant outcome of the action performed by the user within `when` is stated
- **And**: This is used to add an additional condition/result within the `Given`, `When`, and `Then` statements
- **But**: This is used to verify for a negative condition within the `Given`, `When`, and `Then` statements

Following is the example of a test case written in the Gherkin language:

```
Test Case: Select the team and their roster will be displayed
Script -
Given  | Navigate to webpage
Select | "IPL Match" Team
Then | will see the following players:
Number | Name         | Position   | Height    | Weight Pd | Year  |
City
1      | Player1      | Guard      | 5 ft 8 in | 170       | 1     |
City1
2      | Player2      | Forward    | 5 ft 6 in | 165       | 2     |
City2
3      | Player3      | Center     | 5 ft 7 in | 172       | 1     |
City2
4      | Player 4     | Forward    | 5 ft 7 in | 166       | 1     |
City 1
```

Roles of members involved

The following are the roles of the members:

- **Business Analyst**: This member defines the **Acceptance Criteria (AC)** from business perspective in the Gherkin language.
- **Developers**: They identify and analyze the Acceptance Criteria with Scrum team—BA, Testers, and so on.

Feed the Acceptance Criteria in the Gherkin format into tools such as Cucumber for Agile/DevOps BDD.

The BDD tool reads the Acceptance Criteria to generate the Unit tests in the Gherkin format. The developer produces the product source code by running the Unit tests in a Fail-Code-Pass-Done mode.

- **Testers**: They perform the following functions:

Identify and analyze the AC with Scrum team—BA, developers, and so on

Automate AC leveraging on the Acceptance Test automation Framework consisting of the following:

- ○ BDD tool—Cucumber, Gherkin, and so on
- ○ Test framework—Junit, TestNG, and so on
- ○ Interface—Selenium (BDD plugins)
- ○ Integration by means of CI (Jenkins/Hudson)

- Acceptance test scripts are run on the product source code

Benefits of using Gherkin

The benefits of using Gherkin include:

- Requirements can be written as tests. This is especially useful when a business user is writing the requirements for UAT and the language in which it is written doubles up to become a test case.
- Encouraging closer collaboration of IT with business to provide quality output, since business goals are always at the forefront of delivering the projects.
- Duplication of effort in writing the requirements and again rewriting the test cases covering the requirements specified is eliminated.
- Ease of understanding for any layman / business user who wants to understand what functionality is being tested.
- Traceability of the test cases becomes easier, since the requirements and the test cases are the same.
- The specialty of working with Gherkin is that the tests can be written in more than 30 languages, apart from English.

Conclusion

Gherkin provides an *easy to adopt* and *quick to use* approach in terms of a tool used to write test cases for Cucumber, which is one of the most widely used automation tool for executing Acceptance tests in Agile/DevOps BDD. The Gherkin language in Agile/DevOps BDD for test purposes provides a built-in traceability and provides a direct and actionable connection between the requirement artifacts and manual and automated tests. It is very easy to understand for business users, developers, and so on, as to what features are being tested. Hence, Gherkin can be considered as a natural choice for language for acceptance test automation using Cucumber in Agile/DevOps BDD.

14

Automating Configuration Management for DevOps Test Environments

As we discussed in the earlier chapters, use of DevOps is on the rise. DevOps practices enable faster time to market, which is the need of the hour in digital businesses.

DevOps engagements need Test Environments provisioned in a timely manner and with less setup and lead time. It is recommended that the environment configuration management process be automated.

In this chapter, we will cover the following topics:

- Need to automate the test environment configuration process
- Types of Test Environments
- Challenge of Configuration and Environment Management on the Cloud
- Potential solutions for automated Configuration Management
- The benefits of Automated Configuration Management

Background

The transformation of business to a customer-centric digital ecosystem, coupled with the advent of agile and DevOps-based IT processes, has accelerated the adoption of cloud technology solutions.

Migrating the legacy IT systems to the cloud has certain obvious advantages. By supporting global development and decreasing product deployment time, organizations worldwide have been able to roll out product features faster and accelerate the time to market.

From a QA perspective, testers need to be able to quickly verify the testing deliverables. It is important that the setup time for test environments is significantly reduced for cloud-based IT systems. Therefore, both automated test environment setup and on-demand provisioning or removal of test environments are becoming important elements of modern-day software projects. In traditional software development projects, **Configuration Management (CM)** is a manual process for establishing and maintaining the consistency of a platform's functional and physical attributes. In modern day projects, it is essential to have an automated process in which the environment provisioning is done instantly and new environments remain consistent with the previous ones. Configuration management represents a key challenge when implementing a robust test environment management framework on cloud.

Types of test environments

In this section, we will first discuss the various test environment management challenges one may face when migrating IT systems to the cloud. The WQR 2016 suggests that testing happens in permanent, cloud-based, temporary environments; virtualized test environments; and temporary test environments that are not cloud based. Refer to the following graph:

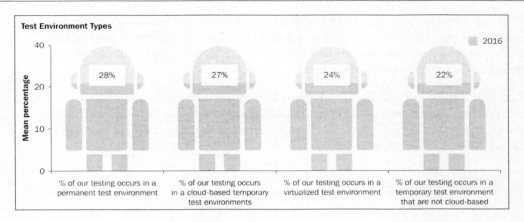

Test Environment Types

Configuration and environment management services on cloud and related challenges

A well-defined configuration management policy plays a very important role in determining the readiness of test environments to move to cloud. The scope of configuration and environment management services comprises of three main actions: defining and implementing configuration management policies, establishing the reference configurations for each environment, and developing a configuration management plan.

The following activities are also considered to be within the scope of test environment configuration management:

- Administering the configuration management toolset
- Monitoring and improving configuration management processes and assets
- Validating and deploying releases
- Promoting configuration from development to testing and staging environments from production to production copies
- Automating the configuration deployment and reporting tasks
- Validating and publishing the release notes

As previously stated, the need for both quick setup time and the on-demand availability of environments is the primary objective of the test environment management discipline.

This requires teams to speed up the deployment process and stabilize the concerned environments. The delay in code promotion from development to testing and to staging environments needs to be reduced through the implementation of automation for code promotion tasks.

According to the World Quality Report 2016, managing multiple versions of ERP test environments remains a major challenge faced by project teams as a result of the consistent lack of automated configuration management of test environments on cloud. Refer to the following diagram:

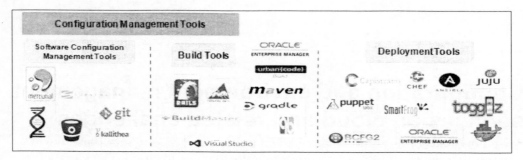

Potential solutions for automated configuration management

To implement an automated configuration management solution, one needs to start by building a configuration management toolset that discovers, reports, and enables actions on operating systems and applications. This toolset automates environment deployment tasks. The configuration management automation ensures the repeatability and consistency of our future environment builds. A configuration management automation toolset is implemented with the steps outlined in the following points:

1. Determine a list of OSes (firewalls, hostnames, and so on) and application configuration items to manage.
2. Install and configure a configuration management tool, such as Puppet, Chef, Salt, or Ansible, for overall configuration management.
3. Install and configure the supporting toolset with Git, Jenkins, and Maven.
4. Generate *as-is* configuration management reports.
5. Build configuration management deployment scripts.
6. Establish a workflow for automated deployments.

7. Document test deployments and procedures.

8. Release deployments and procedures for operational use.

The following diagram provides an insight into the common toolsets used for configuration management automation.

The configuration management toolset includes automated build and deployment tools in addition to configuration.

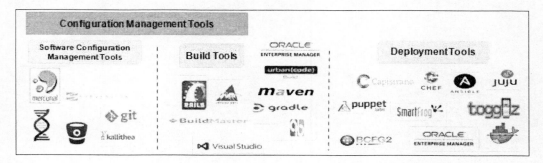

The benefits of automating configuration management

The automation of configuration management activities is required to implement the test environment processes that are compatible with the demands of cloud-based environment provisioning projects. The benefits include the ones listed here:

- Better pipeline management and control, which allows for better asset utilization while lowering **Total Cost of Ownership (TCO)**, management, and support costs

- Increased automation of build and deployment activities, including the use of monitoring (health checks and shakedowns) to improve productivity

Conclusion

In the fast-paced DevOps world, automation of all the required tasks to accelerate time to market holds key importance. Automating the configuration of test environments helps accelerate the DevOps life cycle further. In this chapter, we discussed the specific challenges of environment configuration on cloud, proposed the solutions for automating this activity, and presented the potential benefits.

15

Automated Test Data Management in the DevOps Environment

Automated Test Data Management in DevOps Environment Test Data Management is an important activity in Testing Life Cycle. The quality of testing is only as good as the quality of data with which it is tested. **Test Data Management (TDM)** life cycle steps include definition, discovery, subsetting, masking, validation, and reuse.

To carry out testing effectively, especially in DevOps engagements where the lead-time is of the utmost importance, it is required that the steps in the TDM process are automated.

In this chapter, we will discuss the following:

- Key challenges of test data management in DevOps engagements
- Automated TDM solution for DevOps engagements
- Architecture of TDM solution integrated with DevOps tools
- The benefits of Automated TDM
- Best practices in automated TDM

Background

Consider a large-scale testing project with more than 1,000 business scenarios at the Enterprise level and as many as 10,000 test cases. Such projects are complex and difficult to handle—every phase of software testing is critical and needs the utmost precision and quality. Test data selection and handling it sensitively is critical in such projects. Any breach of customer data has serious consequences for clients and vendors. Test data is a vital component during the execution phase and the data selection exercise requires adequate planning, given the huge volumes of test cases and the complexities involved.

TDM is a process that effectively handles data in complex engagements with the optimal use of resources to enhance the data quality and ensure quality of testing. Test Data provisioning has traditionally been manual, time consuming, and error prone. The limitations of test data include, among others, limited coverage resulting in suboptimal results. Compliance and privacy needs are forcing businesses to relook their test data strategy.

Test data planning and creation should start as early as the test planning phase in the testing life cycle. For large-scale enterprise projects dealing with sensitive customer data, a well-defined test data management process is inevitable.

TDM is a streamlined process used to manage test data end-to-end, that is, starting from its request to its provisioning and including data discovery, data subsetting, data masking, data archiving, data refreshing, and so on, to manage quality and consistent test data across all test environments to perform testing activities.

TDM in DevOps environment – key challenges

In a DevOps environment, the development team requires to deploy the application in order to deliver continuously. To validate the deployed application, it requires a set of quality test data continuously for the execution of integration, functional, and performance testing. Test data provisioning in Continuous Integration / Continuous Deployment is the primary challenge. Key TDM challenges in DevOps environment include the following:

- Test data refreshing in each deployment cycle is a tedious activity.
- Regulatory compliance and data privatization are key challenges to protect sensitive information while deploying data.
- Too many clones of the production environment increase storage costs and cause larger maintenance windows/downtime.

- Test Data Creation is a manual, time consuming, and error-prone process. Lack of knowledgeable resources makes it harder to test packaged applications.

- The overall quality of test data is often poor, causing longer cycle times and suboptimal results.

- Creating subsets of data is not possible without understanding relationships across tables, causing poorer quality test data in CI/CD environments.

Automated TDM solution for DevOps environment

Automated TDM solutions can overcome a number of TDM challenges in DevOps environments and mentioned in the preceding section. Tools that can be considered are as follows:

- Integration — Jenkins
- Version Control — Git
- Build (CI) — MS Build
- Deployment (CD) — MS Deploy
- Test Data Management — IBM Optim/CA Datamaker/Informatica ILM
- QA Automation — UFT and Selenium
- Performance Testing — Jmeter and Load Runner

The process flow to deploy tools includes the following:

- Create end to end automated work flow from version control to performance testing

- Integrate existing test automation (for example, Selenium and UFT) frameworks with CI/CD

- Integrate performance test solutions through Jenkins after the completion of test automation

- Publish the workflow execution status at every stage of the workflow (for example, build success, deployment success, test automation status, and performance test status)

Refer to the following diagram:

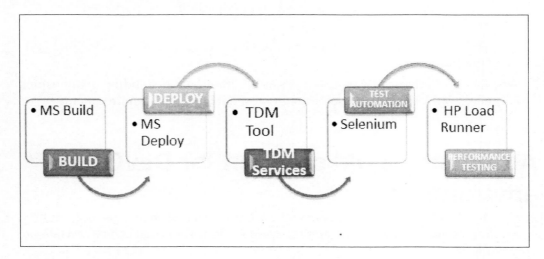

Typical TDM services and TDM architecture

The following are the typical TDM services and TDM architecture:

- **Data Definition**: Build content to drive the TDM process

- **Data Discovery**: Identifies the potentially sensitive or **Personally Identifiable Information (PII)** stored across multiple applications and file formats and provides an accurate picture of the data available, location, and compliance with industry-specific regulations.

- **Data Subsetting**: Creation of smaller copies of data for non-production purposes

- **Data Masking**: Creation of realistic data in non-production environments without risking exposure of sensitive information to unauthorized users and compliance to security guidelines (PII , MNPI, HIPPA, PHI, and so on) without impacting the development process

- **Data Validation**: To ensure data accuracy, completeness, and compliance of TDM processes

- **Data Reuse** — Data can be stored and reused in different cycles

- **Data Refresh** — This is to keep the test environment up-to-date (an ongoing process)

A typical TDM architecture comprises test data sources, synthetic test data generation, a TDM engine with the TDM tool, data subsetting, and masking capabilities, secured test data for testing purposes in repositories, test environments for various tests, and process/method for data validation, as shown in the following block diagram:

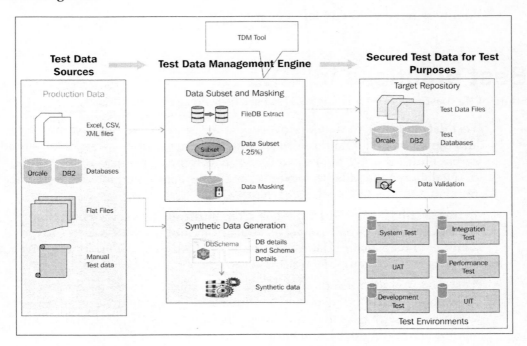

Benefits of automated TDM

The key benefits of the proposed automated TDM solution include the following:

- Optimization of the process, reducing efforts to identify Test Data by 90%
- Reduction in the hours spent waiting for testing environments to be restored, resulting in about a 35% saving
- Reduced subsetting and data masking effort with the use of tools such as ILM Informatica, IBM OPTIM, SAP TDMS, and CA DataMaker
- Right-sized environments and test data aligned to the testing requirements
- Accurate and efficient delivery of TDM data in time
- Cost reduction through reduced storage and infrastructure costs
- Optimal testing coverage

- Ability to track data and its usage
- Masking of production data, and offering production-like quality of test data
- Ability to create synthetic data to meet new testing requirements
- Data creation based on different scenarios
- Ability to run end-to-end test scenarios

Best practices in TDM

Some of the best practices relating to TDM are as follows:

- **Test data analysis or data discovery**: Capture end-to-end business processes and the associated data for testing by identifying sensitive information stored across multiple applications and file formats to provide an accurate picture of the data types available, locations, and compliance with industry-specific regulations.

- **Extract a subset of production data from multiple data sources**: Obtain realistic and referentially intact test data from multiple data sources to create a subset of realistic test databases small enough to support rapid test runs but large enough to accurately reflect the variety of production data.

- **Test data privatization or masking**: Create realistic data in non-production environments without exposing sensitive information to unauthorized users. Compliance with Security guidelines (PII, MNPI, HIPPA, PHI, and so on) without impacting development process.

- **Gold copy of production environment**: Using a gold copy, we can compare baseline data with data that exists in the current test environment. Based on this, new data can be created or the existing data modified as per the business requirements.

- **Test data refresh using gold copy**: Refreshing test data using a gold copy helps improve testing efficiency and streamline the testing process while maintaining a consistent and manageable test environment.

Conclusion

An automated TDM in the DevOps environment helps reduce the risk of data breaches in non-production environments, produce higher-quality test data, streamline development projects, and ensure compliance with data privacy mandates/regulations.

From an overall business impact perspective, an automated TDM process ensures a faster, better, and cost-effective product/solution for the DevOps environments. It helps in maintaining secure and well-integrated test data quality over repeated test cycles. It enhances the overall quality of testing and builds more confidence in generating test data in a CI/CD environment.

16

Testing in DevOps Life Cycle Using Microservices Architecture

Microservices Architecture has gained popularity in DevOps life cycle as it offers a complex application in small modules or system building blocks communicating through APIs.

In this chapter, we will cover the following topics:

- Introduction to microservices architecture
- How is testing carried out in agile/DevOps lifecycle using microservices architecture
- Performance Testing of microservices
- Monitoring of microservices

What is microservices architecture?

Microservices is a software architecture style in which complex applications are composed of small, independent processes communicating with each other using language-agnostic APIs. These services are small building blocks, highly decoupled and focused on doing a small task, facilitating a modular approach to system-building.

Microservice architecture has emerged as a popular response to the shortcomings of traditional monolithic applications. Microservices come with their own set of complexities and concerns. In particular, testing Microservices-based applications requires new approaches to confirm proper operation and continued availability under heavy load in the face of resource failure.

Microservices architecture has become popular in DevOps life cycle.

Testing in agile/DevOps life cycle using Microservices Architecture

To get the most value from unit tests, Microservices tests need to be executed frequently—every build should run the tests. A failed test implies failure of build. Microservices testing should be configured in a continuous integration server (for example, Jenkins, TeamCity, Bamboo) so that these services are constantly monitored for changes in the code.

A testing approach in agile/DevOps life cycle using microservices architecture to provide optimal coverage methodology is highlighted in the following points:

- **Unit Testing**: This will cover basic tests for the API and within each service. Code that uses other services should mock and stub them out.

- **Integrated Testing**: This is to test services from one application to another. Before starting service integration test, test versions of the services that will use the given requests should be created.

- **Performance**: A test system that reflects the production system should be created, which means creating test versions of all the services under test. Volume should reflect real usage.

- **Exploratory testing**: This ties all the services together from an end user perspective.

- **Contract Testing**: This tests the boundaries of the external services to check the input and output of the service calls and validates whether the service meets its contract expectation. Aggregating the results of all the user contract tests helps the developer make changes to a service without impacting the user.

The following diagram depicts how microservices are unit tested. Microservices testing encompasses all tests related to a microservice in isolation. The purpose of these tests is to verify the correctness of the functional integration for all the components that do not require external dependencies. Refer to the following diagram:

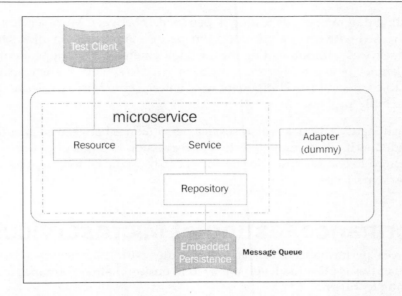

To enable testing in isolation, we typically use mock components in place of the adapters and in-memory data sources for the repositories, configured under a separate profile. Tests are executed using the same technology that incoming requests would use (for example, HTTP for a RESTful microservice).

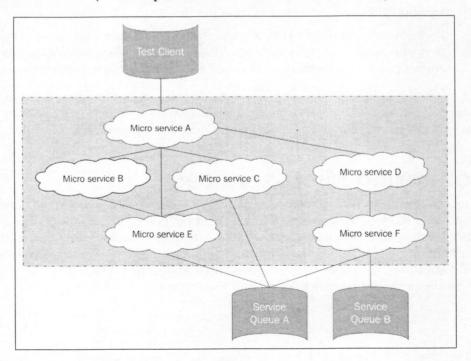

The preceding diagram shows testing dependencies between Microservices that can be addressed with service virtualization. Service virtualization allows testing individual services without waiting for the deployment of other dependent services. Including latency between Microservices tests helps to achieve realistic results. It is important to create and run component tests on each core Microservice and include these in the build process.

Using a dashboard that tracks Microservice performance between each build is also recommended as it allows easy detection of regression in terms of performance. It is also required to test Microservice performance from the UI to guarantee a high-quality user experience.

Performance testing of Microservices

Microservices' performance is crucial and executes performance tests at the unit level rather than at the application level. We need to ensure that performance tests have the following features:

- As realistic as possible and a real dataset should be used
- Load tests should represent the anticipated demand
- Testing should be as close to a realistic production setup as possible
- Microservices should be tested from the cloud using load testing tools
- Performance testing of Microservices is to observe how well the application performs when a high number of calls are made to Microservices or a large amount of data is transferred between individual services on the network

Load testing tools should be used to capture API transactions to scale up the load and monitor the infrastructure. Users can perform such activities on individual Microservices using load testing tools and monitor the infrastructure behavior.

Monitoring Microservices

Microservice architecture introduces a dispersed set of services with higher success as compared to monolithic design that increases the possibility of failures at each service level. A given Microservice can fail due to network issues, unavailability of the underlying resources, and so on. An unavailable or unresponsive Microservice should not bring the whole Microservices-based application down. Thus, microservices should be fault tolerant and should be able to recover.

It is important to be able to detect the failures on a real-time basis, restore the services automatically, and understand the dependencies between the Microservices. We need to ensure that the services are running and performing within a defined set of standards.

Monitoring is a critical piece of the control system of microservices. As the complexity of the software increases, it gets more difficult to understand its performance and troubleshoot the problems. Given the dramatic changes to software delivery, monitoring needs an overhaul to perform well in a microservice environment. The following monitoring steps are recommended:

- Monitor containers and what is inside them
- Set alerts on service performance, not on container performance
- Monitor services that are elastic and multi-locational
- Monitor APIs
- Map monitoring to organizational structure

Leveraging these five principles will help in addressing both the technological and organizational changes associated with microservices.

Conclusion

Testing in microservices architecture can be more challenging than in traditional, monolithic architecture. In combination with continuous integration and deployment, it is even more complex. It's important to understand the layers of tests and how they differ from each other. Only combination of various test approaches can offer confidence in product quality.

17
Automated Test Environments for DevOps

Software testing is carried out on test environments. These are non-production environments that are similar to production environments. Environments are created for various tests: developer (unit) test, dedicated test, integration test, preproduction test, and business readiness test.

Given the time pressures, management of non-production environments does not get priority from IT organizations. There are serious implications of high environment-related defects if test environments are not managed well.

In this chapter, we will cover the following topics:

- Challenges of test environment management (TEM)
- A TEM automation approach for DevOps environments
- Benefits of TEM automation
- TEM metrics to consider for release management
- TEM automation tools

Test Environment Management – key challenges

A testing environment is a setup of software and hardware, in which the testing team tests a new software build. A test environment consists of preproduction or staging environments, and is generally a downgraded version of a production environment to help uncover preproduction defects.

Building and maintaining a test environment are important. Often, dedicated test environments are maintained at various stages like developer test, dedicated test, integration test, and preproduction or business readiness test. Take a look at the following diagram:

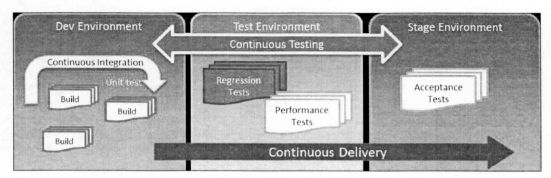

In the rapidly changing business world, an IT organization has to align the IT strategy to business strategy and bring agility into the IT delivery. It is increasingly difficult to manage complex IT infrastructure dependencies and manual intervention becomes unavoidable. Time and again, organizations consider the management of non-production environments as a secondary priority. This leads to unorganized and ad hoc management of test environments and increased operational and maintenance costs for organizations. In addition, identifying and addressing environment-related defects becomes a major concern for QA teams. Effective and efficient management of test environments with structured automation can deliver significant benefits along with substantial cost savings to the organization.

Test environment automation approach for DevOps

Typically, release management is a complex and time consuming process. Even if applications are provisioned using templates, the infrastructure provisioning is often done manually. In a complex DevOps continuous integration environment requiring reduced cycle time for delivering and testing enterprise applications in DevOps methodology, the manual provisioning of environments is not sustainable. Adopting best practices and leveraging automation can drastically improve the cycle time and reduce the time to release without affecting compliance and standards.

An automation framework for environment management in DevOps life cycle includes building and deploying automation for Continuous Development, Continuous Integration, Continuous Testing, and Continuous Delivery. An automation framework caters to automation in the following areas:

- Environment request process
- Environment planning, design, and build provisioning
- Data masking, desensitization, and governance for environment request execution
- Infrastructure baseline and smoke testing

Environment support activities (for example, configuration maintenance and code migrations) can also be automated. Refer to the following diagram:

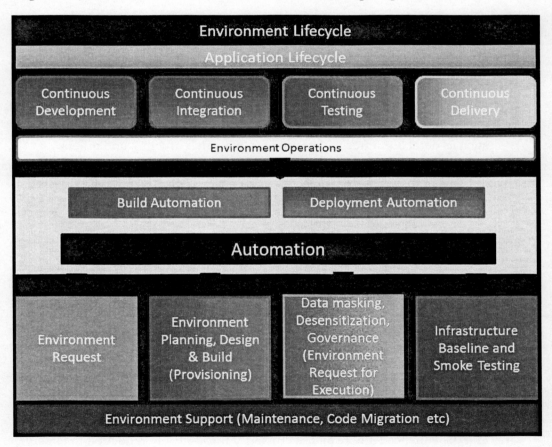

A focused approach toward environment automation can reduce the dependencies involved in manual infrastructure provisioning. Test environment automation approach should support the following activities:

- Environment provisioning, configuration, testing, deployment, and operational management
- Test data management and related compliance requirements
- Proactive monitoring of environment and self-healing for repeat incidents
- Configuration management with auto-discovery for environment asset management and licensing
- Patching and upgrading of infrastructure components compliant with enterprise policies

The approach to test environment automation varies across organizations. Common elements of this approach include a combination of pre-configured tools and scripts supporting the entire environment management life cycle. Once the initial standardization is done, all the inputs, outputs, checkpoints, and failure points in the tasks identified are captured. All the captured items are marked as candidates for local or centralized automation:

- **Localized automation** involves automation limited to specific components, such as database refresh, operating system patch updates, and others
- **Centralized automation** includes the orchestration and integration of various systems in the environment, such as test environment provision requests received through a tool that needs to be executed using a deployment tool and following standard operating procedures

A robust automation script or workflow will lead to the reusability of the scripts that can be used in the future to speed up the provisioning process.

Benefits of test environment automation

The benefits of test environment automation cover the ranges cited in the following points:

- 30-40% reduction in time to market, thanks to an improved provisioning cycle time
- Up to 50% reduction in manual health check efforts
- 20-30% enhanced environment efficiency through 30% reduction in IT service request fulfillment
- 30-40% reduced cost of operations

Additional qualitative benefits of environment management automation include the following ones:

- Elimination of errors due to manual interventions and delays due to dependencies

- Zero tolerance with respect to continuous availability of the environment

- Consistent and accurate environments through automated configuration updates

- Optimum utilization of infrastructure assets through better license management

- Availability of the environment as a service model

Test environment metrics to consider in release management

Key metrics to be considered for the support and management of test environments during release management fall into the following three main categories:

- **Environment efficiency**: This refers to the frequency of environment usage and frequency of conflicts arising out of environment demand. The environments posing regular demand conflicts should be analyzed for impact on release plan. The analysis outcome (for example, test execution stoppage of a release due to the non-availability of the test environment) can help in resolving the conflicts.

- **Environment Stability**: The release cycle or schedule is affected in the case of test environment outages during a release cycle. We need to analyze the outage data, identify the events that impact the stability of specific test environments, and pinpoint those events. The analysis can include the frequency of the environment outage due to project-specific internal factors and external factors. Another area to investigate is the frequency of resorting to a manual workaround due to specific environment issues or outages. Based on this, a plan needs to be created to achieve the critical path for release.

- **Environment Agility**: The speed in which an environment can be created and configured is a measure of its agility. The tasks that need to be modeled and captured in a tool that understands how environments affect releases include environment retooling, so as to match other code branches or releases and system or build validation prereleases.

Test environment automation tools

Some of the commercial tools in test environment automation area are as follows:

- **TEMS**: Plutora's **Test Environment Manager** (**TEMS**) software provides comprehensive preproduction environment management capabilities to service all environment management functions.

- **Chef**: Chef is a configuration management tool used to streamline the task of configuring and maintaining a company's servers and can integrate with cloud-based platforms, such as Rackspace, Internap, Amazon EC2, Google Cloud Platform, OpenStack, SoftLayer, and Microsoft Azure to automatically provision and configure new machines.

- **SmartFrog**: SmartFrog is an open source software framework written in Java, which manages the configuration, deployment, and coordination of a software system broken into components. These components may be distributed across several network hosts.

- **SSH**: Secure Shell, or SSH, is a cryptographic (encrypted) network protocol for initiating text-based shell sessions on remote machines in a secure way. SSH provides administrators with a secure way to access a remote computer for the launch of an instance to test a project version. The SSH protocol is widely used in test environment automation. If development and test environments live inside a **Virtual Machine** (VM), then launching a project version will need SSH authentication keys. Recreating the editor and command line sessions every time you develop and test is a waste of time. A terminal multiplexer allows you to create persistent development sessions running multiple commands in different panes once the SSH key is supplied.

- **Puppet**: Puppet is an open source configuration management utility. It runs on many Unix-like systems as well as on Microsoft Windows and includes its own declarative language to describe system configuration.

- **ServiceNow**: ServiceNow is a **Platform-as-a-Service** (**PaaS**) provider of **Service Management** (**SM**) software for the entire enterprise. It specializes in **IT Service Management** (**ITSM**) applications based on the ITIL standards.

Conclusion

In conclusion, test environment automation allows organizations to streamline repetitive tasks and activities and reduce the overall operation efforts. It follows local and centralized automation approaches to gain more benefits in reducing release time. As a result, it helps organizations to free up resources and then, deploy those resources on other critical activities that aren't developing automation assets.

18

Service Virtualization as an Enabler of DevOps

DevOps engagements have the primary goal of accelerating the time to market. Often, testing is delayed as some of the components in applications may not be available to enable end-to-end testing of an application. Service virtualization can simulate these select components in order to carry out testing without waiting for all the components to be available.

In this chapter, we will discuss the following topics:

- Service virtualization steps in context of DevOps
- Role of service virtualization in DevOps life cycle—popular service virtualization tools

Service virtualization and DevOps

Service virtualization is the process of simulating the behavior of select components within an application to enable end-to-end testing of the application as a whole. Application development teams can use virtual services in lieu of the production or real services to conduct integration testing earlier in the development process.

Virtualized test assets look and act like the real thing but may be duplicated and available at times when the real assets are not available to the testing team. Virtualizing your test assets enables your organization to create robust test frameworks that can provide comprehensive test coverage while keeping costs low.

There are different ways to define DevOps; some of the industry terminologies are listed here:

- A software development method that stresses communication, collaboration, and integration between development and IT professionals
- A set or mix of principles, practices, methods, or concepts
- A combination of development and operations
- A methodology of continuous delivery
- A streamlined release process

DevOps is not only about culture, practices, and methods, it is also about a set of tools that support development, deployment, and operations.

DevOps is the sum of all the tools that pave the way for teams to build, test, and release great software. The fundamental process of service virtualization works like this:

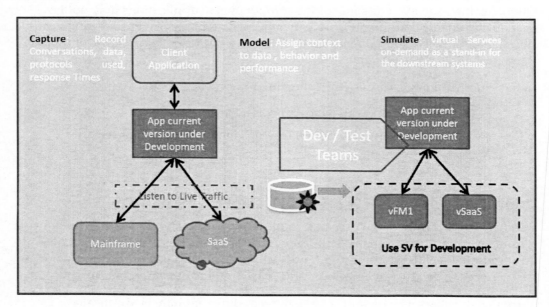

We will explain the architecture in detail in the following lists:

- **Capture**: A *listener* is deployed wherever traffic or messages are flowing between any two systems. Generally, the listener records data between the current version of the application under development and a downstream system that we seek to simulate.

- **Model**: Here, the service virtualization solution takes the captured data and correlates it into a virtual service, which is a *conversation* of the appropriate requests and responses plausible enough for use in development and testing. Sophisticated algorithms are employed to do this correctly.

- **Simulate**: The development team can now use the deployed virtual services on demand as a stand-in for the downstream systems, which will respond to requests with appropriate data just as the real thing would, except with more predictable behaviors and much lower setup cost.

Role of service virtualization in DevOps

DevOps provides a set of principles and practices that enable development and operations teams to communicate and collaborate more effectively. Deploying automation enables the organization to enjoy the benefits of continuous integration and continuous delivery, significantly enhancing both productivity and agility.

Understanding opportunities for acceleration holds the key to process improvement. We need to ensure, though, that acceleration comes without risk to quality.

Software organizations are learning that QA and testing practices must be used throughout the entire software development life cycle. Robust testing practices enable the organization to meet the demands and challenges of continuous delivery. Today, there are methodologies and tools available that help to implement effective testing strategies that meet the demands of even the most complex IT systems embracing DevOps. Refer to the following diagram:

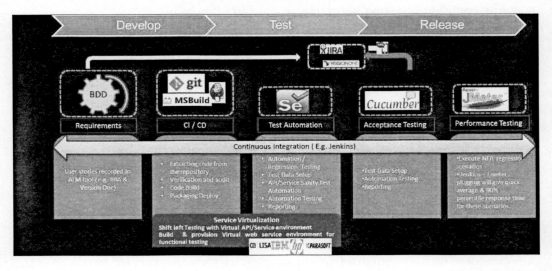

When an organization is looking at *continuous everything*, an emerging best practice known as continuous testing is a critical component in the overall process. Another emerging best practice, known as **Service Virtualization**, enables continuous testing by providing anytime, anywhere access to a complete, simulated test environment.

The recommended capabilities for this goal include an intuitive interface for automating complex scenarios across the messaging layer, ESBs, databases, and mainframes, and touch on the following actions:

- Defining automated test scenarios across the broad range of protocols and message types used in APIs: REST, WADL, JSON, MQ, JMS, EDI, and fixed-length messages

- Automating rich multilayer validation across multiple endpoints involved in end-to-end test scenarios

- Parameterizing test messages, validations, and configurations from data sources, values extracted from test scenarios or variables

- Defining sophisticated test flow logic without requiring scripting

- Visualizing how messages and events flow through distributed architectures as tests execute

With the trend of agile development and increasing system interdependency, it has become extremely difficult to access all the dependent applications. Access to dependent systems and environments is required to execute the necessary type of complete end-to-end tests. By leveraging service virtualization to remove these constraints, an organization can gain full access to the test environment, thereby enabling continuous testing to occur as early and often as needed.

Service virtualization enables rapid iterative development by providing simulated test environments that can help scale continuous testing. The goal of service virtualization is to simulate interfaces and resources that may not always be available for testing due to cost or other constraints. This emerging industry best practice promises to provide a much more robust and comprehensive approach to ensuring that we can continuously deliver error-free code.

Service virtualization – research input

Analysts have been studying company implementation of service virtualization and the results of those implementations for several years. They have repeatedly found that companies using service virtualization experience lower costs, greater software quality, and faster delivery. In fact, the latest research by Gartner, which analyzes a survey of over 500 companies, found that service virtualization led to the following things:

- Dramatically increased test rates with more than a quarter of companies doubling their test execution rates

- More than a third of companies reduced their test cycle times by at least 50 percent

- Nearly half of the respondents saw a reduction of total defects of more than 40 percent

Service virtualization automation tools used in DevOps

The following is a brief overview of the commonly known automation tools used in DevOps:

- **SmartBear**: Automated service virtualization tool similar to ServiceV Pro and Alert site

- **Parasoft Virtualize**: An open automated service virtualization solution; it creates, deploys, and manages simulated dev or test environments. It simulates the behavior of dependent applications that are still evolving, difficult to access, or difficult to configure for development or testing.

- **CA Service Virtualization**: Formerly known as LISA, it captures and simulates the behavior, data, and performance characteristics of complete composite application environments, making them available for development and test teams throughout the software lifecycle for faster time-to-market with quality software functionality at a lower infrastructure cost.

Conclusion

The use of simulation technologies, such as service virtualization, overcomes the constraints associated with the dependent systems outside our control in order to run meaningful end-to-end tests in DevOps. Service virtualization shifts the ability to test applications earlier in the development lifecycle, enabling integration and release processes to happen faster, with higher quality, and lower risk. It also enables other non-functional testing, such as performance testing against a simulated connection, or load testing, simulating multiple connections.

19

Best Practices in Identifying Regression Test Cases

Regression testing is carried out to ensure that changes carried out in an application do not impact the working of the earlier working parts of the application. As the software ages, the size of the test suite keeps increasing.

Regression testing needs to be carried out as many times as a new build is released, even if the changes made are small. In DevOps engagements, where continuous integration is carried out, carrying out manual regression will be time consuming as well as expensive; hence, regression tests are often automated.

It is important to carefully choose test cases that need to be used for regression tests to ensure that a test suite is optimal.

In this chapter, we will discuss the given topics:

- Need for regression testing
- Software regression process
- Process for choosing test cases to be included for regression

Background – software regression testing

Regression testing is carried out to ensure that a system or an **Application Under Test (AUT)** behaves as expected after enhancements or bug fixes. Testing activities occur after software changes and regression testing usually refers to testing activities completed during the software maintenance phase. The key objectives of regression testing include retesting the changed components or parts and then checking the affected parts and components. Regression testing is performed at different levels — unit, integration, functional, and system.

Regression testing is needed for various reasons, such as the following ones:

- Incremental code changes in a project or release
- Major releases or projects going live
- Emergency production fixes
- Configuration and environment changes

Software regression process

The software regression process includes the steps identified in the progression chart, as shown in the following diagram:

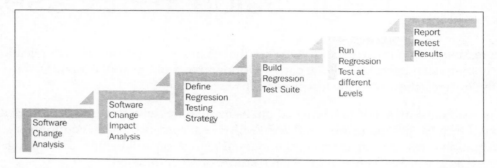

How should one choose test cases for regression?

Choosing test cases for regression packs is not a trivial exercise. There are three types of test suites executed during each release of a software application: regression tests, release specific tests, and defect fix verification tests. Careful thought and attention must accompany the selection of test sets for the regression pack.

The following are some of the guidelines to accomplish this selection exercise:

- **Include the test cases that have frequently yielded bugs**: Some areas in the application are so error-prone that they usually fail following a small coding change. We can keep track of these failing test cases throughout the product cycle and cover them in the regression test suite.

- **Include the test cases that verify the core features of the application**: Prior to designing the test cases, identify all the core features of the application. Ensure that test cases cover all the functionalities mentioned in the requirements document. One can make use of a traceability matrix to ensure that no requirement is left untested.

- **Include the test cases for functionalities that have undergone recent changes**: Maintain the history of functionality changes for test case documentation in order to identify the test cases to include in the regression suite.

- **Include all the integration test cases**: Even if integration testing is a separate part of the software testing cycle, its test cases should be included in the regression test suite. As a last-minute fix, an already-tested application can break the integrity between two different modules. For example, data might get lost across an interface, messages might not get passed properly, or interfaces might not be implemented as specified.

- **Include all the complex test cases**: Some system functionalities may only be accomplished by following a complex sequence of **Graphic User Interface (GUI)** events. To open a file, a user may have to click on the **File** menu and then select **Open**, use a dialog box to specify the filename, and then focus the application on the newly opened window. Obviously, increasing the number of possible operations exponentially augments the sequencing problem. This can become a serious issue; in some scenarios, the whole system's functionality comes to a halt. Hence, all the complex test cases should be part of the regression test suite.

- **Prioritize the test cases for regression testing**: Prioritize the test cases as they relate to business impact and critical and frequently used functionalities. It is always helpful if an analysis is completed to determine which test cases are relevant. One idea is to classify the test cases into various priorities based on importance and customer use. Here, it is suggested that test cases be sorted into three categories:

  ○ **Priority 0**: Sanity test cases check for basic functionality (as per the SRS of the application) and are run to verify presystem acceptance and ensure functionality after an application under test goes through a major change. These test cases deliver high project value.

  ○ **Priority 1**: This includes the test cases that test the essential functionalities for delivering high project value.

  ○ **Priority 2**: These are executed as a part of the system test cycle and are selected for regression testing as needed. These test cases deliver moderate project value.

The selection of test cases based on priority will greatly reduce the efforts spent on regression testing. The following points explain the test cases in detail:

- **Categorize the selected test cases**: Regression testing becomes very difficult when the application scope is large and there are continuous increments or patches to the system. In such cases, selective tests need to be executed in order to save on both testing costs and time. Categorizing test cases makes this work easier. We can place them into two main categories:

  - **Reusable test cases**: These include test cases that can be repetitively used in succeeding regression cycles. This can be automated so that a set of test cases can be easily executed on a new build.

  - **Obsolete test cases**: These are bug-specific and cannot be used in succeeding cycles. The smart way to use them is when the respective bugs occur.

- **Choose the test cases on a case-to-case basis**: There can be several correct approaches to regression testing that must be decided on a case-to-case basis:

  - If the criticality and impact of the bug fixes are low, then it is enough that a test engineer selects a few test cases from the test management tool and executes them. These test cases can fall under any Priority (0, 1, or 2).

  - If the criticality and impact of the bug fixes are medium, then the tester needs to execute all the Priority 0 and Priority 1 test cases. If bug fixes need additional test cases from Priority 2, then those test cases can also be selected and used for regression testing. Selecting Priority 2 test cases in this instance is desirable, but not obligatory.

  - If the criticality and impact of the bug fixes is high, then we need to execute all Priority 0, Priority 1, and carefully-selected Priority 2 test cases. One can also go through the complete log of changes that occur as a result of bug fixes and select the test cases to conduct regression testing. This is an elaborate process, but it can give very good results.

- **Classify regression test cases based on the risk exposure**: The classification of the regression test cases must be performed at the beginning of the project and verified at the closure. Test cases are categorized based on their risk exposure and are calculated based on the scientific logic given here:

Risk Exposure (RE= R x P) = Requirements Risk (R) x Probability for Defect (P)

Probability for Defect (P) = Number of Defects (N) x Average Severity of the Defects (S)

Refer to the following diagram:

Probability for Defect (P) = Number of Defects (N) x Average Severity of the Defects (S)

(N x S)	Probability
9 or higher	3
Between 5 to 8	2
Between 1 to 4	1

Defect Severity	Score
1 (High)	4
2 (Medium)	3
3 (Low)	2
4 (Cosmetic)	1

As depicted in the preceding diagram, higher number of defects per test case (**N**) and/or higher average severity (**S**) of defects in the test case results in a higher **P** score for the test case. Take a look at the following diagram of **Risk Exposure**:

Risk Exposure (RE=R X P) = Requirement Risk (R) * Probability for Defect (P)

Categorization of the regression test cases based on the risk exposure factor as mentioned below.

Risk Exposure	Regression Candidate
9 or higher	Primary
Between 5 to 8	Secondary
Between 1 to 4	Tertiary

Requirement Risk	Score
High	3
Medium	2
Low	1

(N x S)	Probability
9 or higher	3
Between 5 to 8	2
Between 1 to 4	1

As depicted in the preceding diagram, the **Risk Exposure** is a multiplication of the **Requirement Risk** and the **P** value computed earlier. Higher risk exposure test cases with RE value of 9 or above are primary candidates to be included in regression suite; followed by test cases with lower RE values.

Conclusion

Identifying regression test cases is critical and requires complete knowledge of applications or products under test. Change impact analysis and a history of defects both play a major role in the identification of test cases. Therefore, the right combination of testers and business owners can bring value to identify regression test cases in an application's or a product's life cycle. Apart from various criteria for test case inclusion in regression suite, a classification mechanism based on risk exposure score is discussed. Using the risk exposure score, one can classify test cases as primary, secondary, and tertiary for including in regression test suite.

20
Accessibility Test Automation in DevOps Environment

In this chapter we are going to cover the following topics:

- Background – Accessibility (AX)
- AX and DevOps
- AX test automation in DevOps
- Standard AX tools

Background – Accessibility (AX)

Accessibility (AX) testing is a subset of usability testing. In accessibility testing, users under consideration include people with disabilities as well. The significance of this testing is to verify both usability and accessibility. Considering the range of issues people may be dealing with, it is important to build applications that everyone can use. There are standards that have been established to address this need (section 508) and **Web Contact Accessibility Guidelines (WCAG)**. Refer to the following diagram:

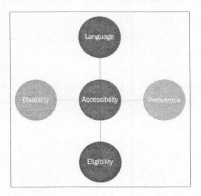

AX and DevOps

In order to adapt to a continuous delivery in DevOps, AX testing needs to be considered in the early phases of the project. The scope of accessibility testing should be finalized in the design phase, and the test strategy should be finalized after this. The tools that can support this should also be considered early in the life cycle. Refer to the following diagram:

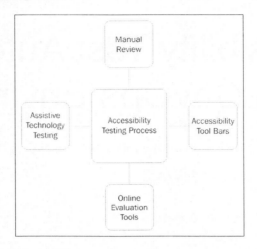

It is generally not possible to automate all the accessibility test cases. Even the best automated accessibility testing can only verify 25% of WCAG checkpoints and even then, the results are assessed manually. In order to build automated accessibility tests in a continuous integration test suite, only tests that are 100% objective need to be included. Covering 10% of WCAG checkpoints is considered good while automating AX testing.

AX test automation in DevOps

It has become essential to test early in the development process to find and correct accessibility conformance issues. This offers the potential to save valuable time and cost, especially because it can be used as a way to provide feedback to the development team so that the issues are taken into consideration at an early stage of implementation. With automated AX tests, accessibility concerns can be identified and remediated prior to releasing the code to the test team.

Chapter 20

Automated testing tools give developers a complete view of accessibility issues, such as alternative text and color contrast. AX tools recommend necessary corrections that improve the user experience. The AX tools help with adherence to accessibility standards and government regulations (Web Content Accessibility Guidelines, US Section 508, Americans with Disabilities Act).

There are many tools available to help ensure accessibility of applications. Some of these include:

- Web developer toolbars in browsers to disable CSS and check for logical reading orders (the non-CSS view is basically what will be read with a screen reader)

- Browser add-ons that reveal the underlying accessibility information (such as WAVE for Firefox or Chrome)

- Desktop tools such as Color Oracle to help simulate colorblindness

- Screen readers that read the screen to you (people are mostly familiar with JAWS or VoiceOver for a desktop screen reader, but have you tried the accessibility options on your phone?)

Many of these tools are simple to use and don't add a lot of overhead if some checks are done early in the development process.

Standard AX tools

Some of the industry standard tools in AX space include:

- **ATF-WAVE web accessibility solution**: Captures the HTML of each unique page of application navigated via WebDriver, and then fires the Wave accessibility tool. We then check the DOM to ensure that there are no WAVE errors and screenshot it and fail the test if there are. This is all done during a dedicated accessibility stage of your build pipeline.

- **IBM digital content checker**:
  - Allows anyone to easily upload and verify the accessibility of HTML content or EPUB documents so that clients, employees, and constituents encounter no issues when accessing the information in web and mobile applications
  - Quickly examines the content, provides a detailed report of all accessibility violations, and then recommends how to fix the issues so that the content conforms to the standards and regulations before it is published

        ◦   Can be customized for an organization's internal content
            development workflow, so accessibility is part of the review
            and approval process

- **IBM automated accessibility tester**: Incorporates automated accessibility
  reporting and auditing capabilities directly within the Selenium testing
  framework. This improves the quality of the testing environment by
  adding accessibility checkpoints that run during agile development,
  so any violations can be corrected in DevOps before deployment.

Conclusion

Accessibility has become a critical focus area for organizations worldwide in order
to improve the user experience on any device, optimize communications, satisfy
compliance requirements, and to create an inclusive workplace environment.
Organizations are finding better ways to integrate accessibility across the entire
enterprise — from the design, development, and testing of applications to any
content that is published on websites. Automating accessibility tests ensures
early completion of tests and, in turn, faster release to market.

21
Performance Tuning of Java Applications

The goal of performance analysis in any Java-based application is to determine which parts of a program require optimization to increase their execution speed or lower their memory usage. Performance analysis is used for the following things:

- Pro-active bottleneck identification
- Application profiling
- Fixing scenarios that are not meeting requirements/SLAs

Based on performance analysis, bottlenecks can be identified and performance tuning can be carried out.

In this chapter, we will discuss the following topics:

- Performance bottlenecks in applications and key challenges posed by these
- Solutions for resolving bottlenecks, for example, object reuse, delayed initiation, and so on
- Performance tuning tools for Java applications, for example, Netprofiler

Performance bottlenecks – key challenges and solutions

A bottleneck can be any factor that prevents the system from meeting the performance target; it is a resistance to the flow of data. Bottleneck can be within any layer of the technology stack or the infrastructure. The bottlenecks in application layers can pertain to objects/methods. The bottlenecks at database level can pertain to queries and locks. The hardware bottlenecks relate to processor, IO layer, memory, and network layer.

Two major performance problems in Java applications include excess creation of objects or excess collection of garbage.

Objects need to be created before they can be used and garbage should be collected when they are finished with.

The more objects you use, the more garbage-cycling happens, the CPU cycle wasted

Each object creation is roughly as expensive as a *malloc* in C, or a *new* in C++, and there is no easy way of creating many objects together, so you cannot take advantage of efficiencies you get using bulk allocation.

For example, a person object that holds a name object, consisting of a first name, last name and an address object, with street, number, and so on. These three objects can be collapsed down to the person object with all the fields moved up to the person class.

Performance tuning in Java involves reusing objects, managing a pool of objects, canonicalizing objects, enumerating constants, comparison with identity, and avoiding excess garbage collection.

We will now discuss each of these techniques briefly in this section.

Reusing objects

Following are the resources we required to reuse the objects and make things more efficient:

- Objects are expensive to create, so it is reasonable to reuse the same object.
- This requires awareness of when not to create a new object.
- Look at the object and consider whether it is possible to reset the fields and then reuse the object, rather than throwing it away and creating another.
- Important for objects that are constantly used and discarded; for example, in graphics processing, objects such as rectangles, points, colors, and fonts are used and discarded all the time. Recycling these types of objects can certainly improve performance.

Managing pool of objects

While not using the retained objects, we are holding on to more memory than if we simply discarded those objects, and this reduces the memory available to create other objects.

Balance the need to have some free memory available against the need to improve performance by reusing objects.

The space taken by retaining objects for later reuse is significant only for very large collections, and you should certainly know which ones these are in your application.

Canonicalizing objects

Canonicalizing objects of replacing multiple copies of an object with just a few objects is often referred to as canonicalizing objects. Consider the following example:

```
Boolean t1 = new Boolean (true);
System.out.println(t1=!Boolean.TRUE);
System.out.println(t1.==(Boolean.TRUE));
produces the output: False OR True
```

Enumerating constants

Another canonicalization technique often used is replacing constant objects with integers; this is called **Enumeration**. Enumeration can provide both speed and memory advantages. The enumeration requires less memory than the equivalent strings and makes network transfers faster. Rather than using the female and male strings, we should use a constant defined in an interface.

Comparison versus identity

Comparisons are faster compared to identity and can be used instead of the equality comparison.

For example, we can use `this.gender == FEMALE;` instead of `this.gender.equals("Female");`.

Avoiding excess garbage collection

The canonicalization techniques are one way to avoid garbage collection; fewer objects means less to less garbage to collect.

The pooling technique tends to reduce garbage-collection requirements, partly because you are creating fewer objects by reusing them, and partly because you deallocate memory less often by holding on to the objects you have allocated.

Reducing garbage collection by using primitive data type is when you hold an object in a primitive data type format rather than another format as primitive data type uses less memory.

Delayed initialization

Technique of delaying object creation until the last possible moment is useful for avoiding unnecessary object creation when only a few objects are used although many possible objects can be created.

Many objects need to be created and initialized and most of these objects will be used, but not immediately. In this case, it is useful to spread out the load of object initialization so that you don't get a large hit on the application. It may be better to let a background thread initialize all the objects slowly or to use lazy initialization to take many small or negligible hits, thus spreading the load over time.

Java performance tuning tools

There are many tools available in the market to analyze and monitor Java applications that help us to find which part of the code should be optimized. Some of them are as follows:

- NetBeans profiler for analyzing java application
- JAMon, Java Application Monitor
- GCViewer, which visualizes verbose garbage collection data generated by Sun and IBM **Java Virtual Machines (JVM)**
- HPjmeter , which is specific to Methods/Object
- HPjtune—JVM

NetBean profiler for analyzing Java applications

The NetBeans profiler is a powerful tool that provides important information about the runtime behavior of an application. The NetBeans profiler helps in tracking the following things:

- Thread state
- CPU performance
- Memory usage
- Object creation
- Method creation

Thread state

Threads (Timeline) shows the current and historical thread state, updated as the application runs.

Threads (Details) shows a summary of the thread state information for a single thread.

Refer to the following screenshot:

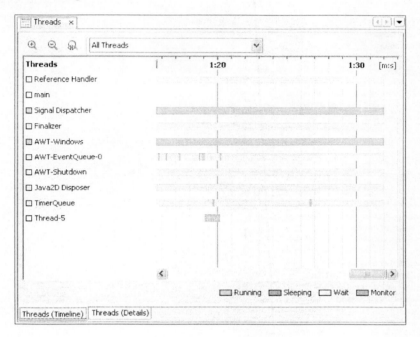

Following are the Thread states:

- **Green**: The thread is either running or is ready to run
- **Purple**: The thread is sleeping; for example, it is called `Thread.sleep()`
- **Yellow**: The thread is waiting in a call to `Object.wait()`
- **Red**: The thread is blocked while trying to enter a synchronized block or method

CPU Performance

This tool has a CPU snapshot that contains the following tabs:

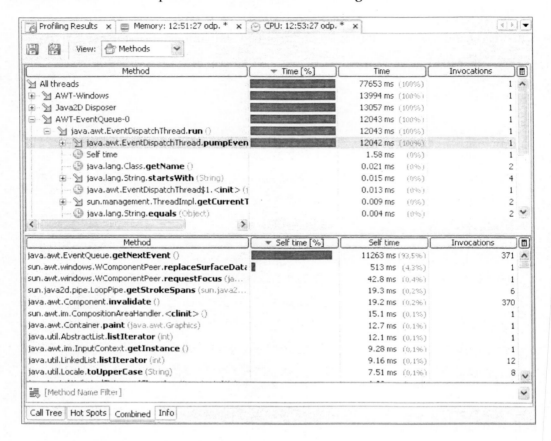

Let's see how the particular tree and spot works:

- **Call Tree Displays the Calling Context Tree (CCT)**, showing the method call chain and the time/number of invocations for executing threads and methods in each context (a context is a unique chain of method calls leading to the method's invocation.)

- **Hot Spots** shows the total execution time and number of invocations for each method, irrespective of the context.

Memory Usage

Memory usage is one of the most vital process in any system. Next, we will see how thing works with the help of following screenshot:

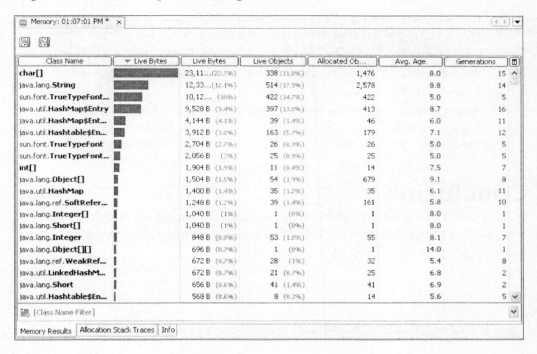

Preceding screenshot gives a more information on how memory usage happen with the help of class name and live bytes. Next screenshot would be more about the output of various data all together:

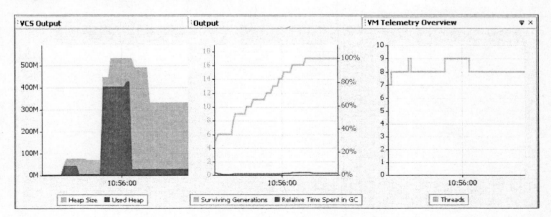

The tool snapshots contain the following tabs:

- **Allocated Objects**: The number of objects that the NetBeans profiler is actually monitoring.

- **Live Objects**: The number of the **Allocated Objects** that are still on the JVM's heap and are therefore taking up memory.

- **Live Bytes**: The two columns show the amount of heap memory being used by the **Live Objects**. One column displays a graph and the other displays text.

- **Average Age**: This value is calculated using the live objects. The age of each object is the number of garbage collections that it has survived. The sum of the ages divided by the number of **Live Objects** is the average age.

Conclusion

We discussed various techniques, processes, and tools involved in performance tuning of Java applications with some illustrations. A similar concept can be extended to other development platforms as well.

22
Testing Mobile Applications – Key Challenges and Considerations

With increased mobility and increased m-commerce, organizations spend significant time trying to understand consumer needs. Consumers have more and more data at their disposal to be able to make decisions. This has led to changed behaviors of consumers and ever increasing expectations. The end result is changed market dynamics of how we do business.

More and more enterprises are leveraging mobility to boost their top-lines, improve efficiencies, and venture into new business areas and penetrate the markets.

Today, millions of mobile users depend on their devices and mobile apps. Mobile users are increasingly becoming critiques of user experience and the performance of mobile apps. Increased usage of mobile apps has also increased the need for robust testing of these applications before releasing them to the market.

In this chapter, we will discuss the following things:

- Key expectations from end users.

- Key challenges encountered in testing mobile applications; for example, user experience, contextual appropriateness, varied user interfaces, device availability, time to market, and so on.

- Potential solutions.

User expectations

Increase of digital business has come along with increased expectations of the customers. Users expect the following things:

- Increased services
- To share experience with retailers they like
- Personalized and relevant content
- More help and ideas about the product they like
- To research online and seek reviews and advice
- To buy from wherever they want
- Unique offers
- Lifestyle solutions

Refer to the following diagram:

Chapter 22

Key challenges encountered in testing mobile applications

Lets' discuss the key challenges encountered in the use of mobile applications as well as the challenges in testing these applications. It is required that common challenges faced by mobile app users are addressed during the testing of these applications.

User experience

Success of mobile applications is primarily determined by user experience. User experience includes ease of navigation, speed of response, and defect-free transactions. User experience can be enhanced further with innovative and contextually appropriate experience. It is important to ensure that the existing bugs are addressed and new bugs are not regressed to prevent poor end user experience.

Contextual appropriateness

Context can limit or extend the operation of mobile applications or its functionalities. Types of smartphones denote changed environments and usage patterns that impact context. Contextually appropriate data from the environment can enhance customer experience. Contextually, different data and testing creates a unique challenge in the testing process.

Varied mobile user interfaces

Different mobile operating systems like Android, Windows, and so on have different user interfaces, which in turn are guided by specific rules and guidelines. The usage and layout of elements is checked in the verification process when you publish the mobile applications in the markets. Non-compliance with rules and guidelines can delay the publishing process, leading to an increase in the cost of development and testing in turn.

Device diversity and availability

The number of the devices to be tested for compatibility is huge, especially Android. Availability of all physical devices for different regions is high risk and investment. Remote testing adds more complexity to this aspect.

Device based testing approach

Under the device-based approach, there should be a testing laboratory set up, which also involves purchase of real-time mobile devices. It seems to be costlier than the emulation method as it takes care of verification of device-based functions and other quality of service parameters. This method needs to cope with the rapid changes in the ever changing mobile devices and platforms.

Automated testing of layouts

Automated tested involves loading pages and images in renderer and comparing the output with the expected results. This is much beyond just layout and rendering and includes pixel-level test for image rendering and positioning. The test should be targeting the smallest possible code fragment or feature. Layout test spans across browsers and devices applications; hence, visual and rendering responsiveness testing should be one of the key testing considerations.

Test automation challenges with non-standardized tools

Mobile Automation is evolving and there are a variety of tools available in the market and an Automation solution that runs across platforms/OSes/devices is the need of the hour. There are tools specifically meant for platforms, such as iOS and Android. Using a tool that is meant for iOS (for example, Frank for iOS) when you needed to test for both iOS and Android would be considered *non-standard*. The right tool selection and creating a robust framework is the challenge to be addressed.

Reduced time to market

Shrunken timelines to release the applications reduces the available time for testing. Ample time needs to be planned for effective testing and release. Security issues' apps and devices managed via private cloud are much more secure than apps running in a public cloud. A secure private cloud can provide all the access to testing teams and there would be no data breaches whatsoever.

Recommendations to enhance mobile applications usability

Some of the key recommendations to enhance the usability of mobile applications include the following things:

- Test early, test often
- Test competitor products before developing your product
- Test wireframe early in the development process
- Test user journeys through live users for real customer experience
- Conduct cross-browser/cross-screen tests
- Test on multiple platforms

Conclusion

With increased proliferation of devices being used by consumers, m-commerce is a reality. Consumers want seamless business using the variety of gadgets available today. Increased customer expectations and a variety of devices and platforms on which business is conducted has specific challenges for mobile testing. In this chapter, we discussed the challenges faced in testing mobile applications. These challenges can be addressed by testing early, keeping an eye on competitive products, and getting involved in testing them even while your product is under development. In testing mobile applications, focus has to be on end-to-end customer journey validation using multiple browsers and platforms. Automation tools in cross-browser/cross-platform testing have made these challenges easier to handle.

23
Testing Analytics Applications – What Has Changed in SMAC World

Social media has revolutionized the way we interact and has also changed the way we do business. Social media has enabled people to listen to, create, share, comment, and exchange information in virtual communities and networks with speed. It has allowed access to anything and anyone from anywhere.

Social media evolution has offered the customers an end-to-end experience in the buying process. The customers are able to check products from various providers online as well as in stores, touch and feel the features, check feedback from other buyers, order and pay through multiple channels, and so on. Effective use of social media has enabled businesses to improve **Net Promoter Score (NPS)**, brand impressions and sustainability of the customer relationships, resulting in higher customer satisfaction.

In this chapter, we will cover the following topics:

- Understanding the customer and gathering and analyzing data about customers
- Testing the data
- Testing business intelligence and analytics applications
- Testing big data applications—What is unique about them

Understanding your customers, gathering data and analyzing it

In order for a business to reach out to its customers, it is important to first understand the customer. Some of the key questions to understand customers include 4 Ps and 1 C:

- **Person**: Who are my customers?
- **Place**: Where are those customers located?
- **Product**: What are their likes and dislikes?
- **Preferences**: Why do they have specific preferences?
- **Channel**: How to reach them?

Businesses gather enormous data in order to answer the preceding questions. Once one has access to such data, analysis of volumes of data is required to understand and enrich customer experience.

Testing the data

Testing for these volumes of data requires analytics applications to gather, analyze, interpret, and present content from multiple channels, including web and mobile.

Testing analytics applications requires exploration of **social media, mobility, analytics, and cloud (SMAC)** world. It involves gathering customer data from social and mobile channels, leveraging the data, and storing it in cloud platforms. The three key characteristics of data include volume, variety, and the main challenge to address in testing analytics application involves validating the 6Vs.

Characteristics of data to be tested and testing to be done includes the following things:

- Data volumes (Test for semantics, distributed processing, and scalability)
- Data variety (Test for visualization, schemas, and data federation)
- Data velocity (Test real-time, on the fly integration and on-demand storage)

In addition to bearing in mind the volumes, variety, and velocity of the data to be tested, the testing should be carried out for the following things:

- Test for validity of data (apply rules and remove invalid data)
- Test for variability in data (inconsistency)
- Test for veracity of data (quality/accuracy)

Data gathering is usually done using data mining techniques and text mining. Once data is gathered, we employ machine learning techniques to present the data. The data is then tested for the preceding 6Vs.

In each of the earlier steps – gathering, presentation, and testing, there is scope for automation, analytics (descriptive, predictive, and prescriptive). The complexity increases further with increased channels utilized across web and mobile.

Testing the BI/BA applications

Need for quicker analytics, use of social media, and mobility applications has led to use of agile business intelligence technologies, such as big data and Hadoop, where need for faster change adoption is driving the use of agile methods.

Analytics solutions should be tested for common testing techniques, such as security testing, performance testing, usability testing, and custom techniques such as failover testing.

- **Security testing**: To focus on authorization and authentication of users, and availability of data, session permissions, application flow, and other required security tests.

- **Performance testing**: To focus on accuracy of data and performance under high load.

- **Usability testing**: To check whether the application is providing right information, for example, providing a single view of customer from multiple data sources.

- **Failover**: To ensure that data is available during critical failures if the application reaches a predefined threshold.

How is testing done differently for big data/Hadoop applications?

How has testing changed with evolution of big data (as compared to testing enterprise data warehouse)?

One of the angle to it is the increasing use of big data over cloud, resulting in increased convergence of *Analytics* and *Cloud*.

I would like to offer a viewpoint based on three criteria – data, platform, and infrastructure and validation tools:

- **Software and data**: Big data applications work with unstructured/semi-structured data (dynamic schema) and compared to static schema with which EDW applications function. Hence, while EDW applications can do with testing based on sampling, big data applications need to test the population. Testing the data for volume, variety, and velocity here means testing for semantics, visualization, and real-time availability of data, respectively.

- **Platform**: Since big data applications are hosted on cloud (platform as a service), the applications need to be tested for ability of *distributed processing* and to ensure *integration on the fly* without availability of formal data schemas in EDW world.

- **Infrastructure**: Big data applications do not have limitation of linear growth of data as the data can be stored in multiple clusters through **Hadoop Distributed File systems (HDFS)**, a reliable shared storage system that can be analyzed using MapReduce technology. There is an exponential increase in the number of requirements to be tested; hence, test suites need to be based on reuse and optimization, else face maintenance disaster. In case of EDW, storage is based on file systems and linear growth of data. Refer to the following diagram:

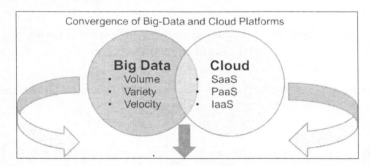

	Volume	Variety	Velocity
Software as a Service (SaaS)	Semantics	Visualization	Real-time
Platform as a Service (PaaS)	Distributed Processing	Schema-less	Integration on the fly
Infrastructure as a Service (IaaS)	Scalable Store	Federated Store	On-Demand Store

- **Validation tools**: In the big data world, there are not many defined tools yet. Use of programming tools, such as MapReduce, that support coding in Perl, Java, Ruby, and Python, and wrappers like HIVE QL built on MapReduce is common. In EDW world, the validation tools are based on SQL, use of Excel Macros, and UI.

So, an opportunity to do independent testing in big data world involves validating the following things:

- Whether requirements are mapped to the correct data sources and if any data sources have been missed out

- Whether structured and non-structured data is stored at the right places, without duplication, and whether there are any data synchronization needs

- Whether test data is created with correct schema and whether the same can be replicated more easily using tools

- Whether the system is behaving as expected when cluster is added or removed

Conclusion

What has changed for analytics testing in SMAC world?

To address the testing for big data, one needs to understand the system and prepopulate data in the system. Testers need to create installations to be able to carry out real-time tests.

There are not many testing tools for big data; the testers are learning basic components of big data to be able to use big data design and development tools (the same as developers) to be able to test big data. Tools such as query surge can help test up to 100% data quickly.

Experience in testing EDW applications has helped shorten the learning curve for testers testing big data as they apply the knowledge of extract, transform, and load from DWH to the Hadoop HDFS.

24
Migrating Applications to Cloud Environments – Key Testing Considerations

Today, more and more organizations are hosting their applications on cloud environments. Organizations are strategically migrating to cloud-ready applications. Also, most new development projects in social media, analytics, cloud, mobility, and IOT are being developed on the cloud.

Depending on the industry and regulatory requirements, the choice of cloud can vary: public, private, and hybrid.

The key drivers include the following ones:

- Need to consolidate geographically spread data centers to a single cloud environment
- Reduce upfront infrastructure investment
- Ease of availability and ease of disaster recovery
- Ease of scaling up/down

In this chapter, we will discuss the following things:

- Need for validating applications for cloud migration
- Key testing focus areas in migrating applications to cloud
- Key challenges in validation during cloud migration of applications (for example, integration, security, and environment compatibility)
- A holistic approach to validating cloud migration

Need for validating applications for cloud migration

While the benefits of cloud hosting are compelling, there is a need to assess the migration plan and carry out the required validation to ensure successful transition. One would ask what additional or different validation needs to be carried out while migrating an application hosting to cloud?

The validation objectives, approach, and rigor can vary based on whether the application is native on the cloud or migrated from physical servers.

For a large number of applications migrated, the validation plan needs to be aligned to migration plan. The tools/accelerators should be used for validation.

Criticality and complexity of application including any compliance requirements.

Key testing focus areas in cloud migration of applications

Migrating applications to cloud requires a formal validation for functional, integration, security, scalability, and performance aspects. Cloud hosting adds new dimensions to application validation as compared to conventional testing. The following table highlights the specific focus areas of testing of applications migrated to cloud as compared to traditional testing:

Testing focus	Traditional Testing	Cloud Testing
Functional validation	• Validating component functions and system functions as well as service features	• SaaS/Cloud service functions end-to-end application functions
Integration Testing	• Function-based integration • Component-based integration • Architecture-based integration • Interface/connection integration	• SaaS-based integration in a cloud • Enterprise-oriented application integration between SaaS/Cloud and with legacy system
Security testing	• Function-based security features • User privacy • Client/server access security • Data/message integrity	• SaaS/Cloud security features, including monitor and measurement • User privacy in diverse clients • Data security during transit and storage • SaaS/Cloud API and connectivity security
Scalability & Performance Testing	• Performed in a fixed test environment • Online monitor and evaluation	• Performed in a scalable test environment • Online monitoring, validation, and measurement

Key challenges in validation during cloud migration of applications

Some of the challenges in validation for cloud migration include the following ones:

- **Application security**:
    - ° Lack of testing and quality of service standards that address cloud and SaaS security.
    - ° Different aspects for application security testing include testing of the following things:
    - ° Data security
    - ° Application transaction security
    - ° Business process security
    - ° User privacy
    - ° Application performance
    - ° Public clouds are shared by multiple users and this can pose bandwidth issues in access or cause outages

- **Integration testing**: Lack of control on the underlying environment (network, database, and servers).

In the case of interactions between network, database, and servers, there is increased challenge as the tester will need to assess the risk of crash, network breakdown, and defunct server.

- **Environment compatibility**: Certain servers and storage or network configurations may not be supported on cloud. It makes it difficult to emulate cloud environments.

Application migration validation – a holistic approach

It is important to verify that all aspects of the migrated application are performing as expected for the application to be certified as **Cloud Ready**. The following checklist with validation for key objectives can be handy to assess the production readiness of migrated applications:

- **Application availability for use**: Validate whether the authorized users can access the application and its services.

- **Response-time as per SLAs**: Validate whether the application and service performance under various loads is meeting the SLA consistently over a period of time.

- **Environment and data management**: Validate whether the application reference data, master data, and the transaction data is transitioned to cloud.

- **Application functioning**: Validate whether each component of each application functions as expected.

- **Automated lifecycle management**: Validate whether application instance is restored automatically in case of hardware failures. Also, whether application data is restored automatically in case of crashes.

- **Application coordination with environment**: Validate whether application is well coordinated and configured to ensure redundancy and failover.

- **Data management**: Validate cloud providers' ability to meet compliance requirements relating to data. Validate data security during transit and storage.

- **Disaster recovery and business continuity**: Validate the backup plan in the event of cloud outage. Validate the business continuity plan for business critical functions in case cloud cannot be accessed.

- **Protection of data property rights**: Validate whether private cloud provider has the right to access data

- **Security of application and data assets post transition**: Validate whether security controls have been enlisted, verified, and evaluated and validate the encryption of sensitive data and remote connections.

Conclusion

Testing objectives/validations and approaches should be carefully considered based on the target cloud platform.

Testing challenges should be carefully examined and addressed.

Testing objectives/validations vary based on application criticality/type, type of target cloud, and whether the application is native to the cloud or has migrated to cloud.

A validation checklist should be deployed for each application migrated to be cloud-ready for production usage.

25

How Should a Tester Adapt to Cloud – Call for Change of Mindset among Testers

The dawn of the digital era brings a new set of challenges for companies today. With cloud, mobile, analytics, and social media forming the cornerstones of digital transformation initiatives, unanticipated obstacles often appear along the road to digitization. These digital roadblocks may stall the overall digital evolution, sending developers back to the drawing board to draft alternate routes around the problem. Finally, these obstacles may actually be the product of individuals seeking to bring such digital initiatives to life.

In the past, testers have relied on well-maintained applications and a scope of testing limited to both functionality and the ability to scale. The traditional way of testing was to work on requirements, create a test strategy, design test cases, and then execute them in a closed environment. This testing almost always lacked certain infrastructural components; such elements were considered a function of in-house IT teams and therefore taken care of whenever the need arose. Testers hardly considered security, as most of the application-hosting infrastructure—servers, firewalls, and ingress or egress points—were under direct control of the enterprise itself. Tester tasks were, therefore, confined to verifying that the new functionality was available in the migrated environment, that it worked as designed, and that it could scale to the demands of end users.

Cloud brings in scenarios and uncertainties that were previously ignored or deemed trivial. In the earlier chapters, we discussed key considerations for testing the cloud migration of applications. Refer to the following diagram:

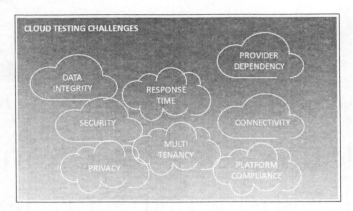

In this chapter, we will take a look at the need for change in the mindset of company individuals pursuing digital transformation. It is important that all stakeholders be prepared to ensure the success of transition. We will examine an enterprise taking the first step towards transformation by moving an on premise application to a cloud platform and what this means to a test team responsible for validating the success of the overall migration.

With enterprises now embracing cloud solutions for application hosting, test teams must know how to address the new realities of testing in the cloud environment.

What must testers prepare for when testing applications on cloud

In the past few years, IT has witnessed an evolution of virtualization in the form of cloud computing. Any novice to cloud must picture cloud computing as a model that views everything *as a service*. The following are the firm requirements of testing application on cloud:

Testing the invisible

Testing on the cloud demands a fundamental change in the tester's mindset. The confidence and reassurance provided by on premise solutions is no longer available. The tester now needs to test something that cannot be seen but exists somewhere in the network. Also, testers do not have the liberty or convenience of making hardware and software changes as before. Therefore, careful planning and collaboration with the cloud support team is crucial. Following this changed perspective, testers must be better prepared to both test and address the ambiguities that come from not being able to see the platforms that host the applications under test.

Understanding the distance

Cloud solutions can include applications hosted by third-party providers, such as AWS, Microsoft Azure, and others. There may also be instances of private clouds within an organization that are located at a centralized data center or even public clouds that may host non-sensitive data. It is essential for testers to realize that the application under test will not be co-located. This brings in another aspect of *latency*, or the time taken for a response to reach or arrive from the point a command is issued by the tester. In on premise applications, latency is typically insignificant and is a factor of the WAN bandwidth available in the enterprise. In cloud, applications are hosted on platforms that may be far from test teams. As a result, the links or paths that connect them may also incur a significant amount of latency. In many large enterprises, data centers hosting applications can be on different continents. Thus, testing in these scenarios requires a recalibration of tester response time expectations. A tester should be able to raise a flag if the response time is slower than with on premise applications.

Breaking the communication barriers

Distance itself brings in a new aspect of communications. Problems arising due to communication were trivial for on premise applications as all teams were co-located. Resolution was just a matter of a coffee break discussion, an informal phone call, or a friendly chat. This may not be the case with the cloud as it may be maintained by another provider or by a geographically separated team. In this case, it is of utmost importance that the testers communicate in the best possible manner, look inward, and take adequate measures to resolve this otherwise nonexistent bottleneck.

Securing the application

Applications hosted on the cloud need not be on premise — they can be hosted on other platforms at a distance. With this design, the need for secure access, self-containment, and code quality becomes important. Cloud platforms are designed to house applications on a tenancy basis; this may also include applications that belong to other enterprises. In such a situation, concerns about privacy, integrity, and security take precedence over functionality. It is, therefore, extremely important for a tester to ensure that an application is secured by performing a security assessment of the path and cloud containers along with the application code itself. Testers need to understand the security risks and consequences that the organization may experience in cases of neglect.

Replicating the platform

Traditional test environments mimicked the production environment. Testers did not need to worry about the performance, scalability, and stability of a project as long as platform specifications were maintained. However, when it comes to applications hosted on the cloud, this may not be the case. Cloud platforms are typically designed and built to support multiple applications using widely available commodity hardware, such as servers and storage arrays, to make them commercially viable. Hence, when testers test applications hosted on the cloud, the underlying platform also plays a vital role. Testers need to ensure that the cloud platform demonstrates the same performance requirements as an on premise solution. Therefore, the ability to translate performance readings to enterprise benchmarks is critical.

Using the right tools

The on premise model allowed the tester to select the tool of their choice for testing. There were hardly any challenges with the test data stored by these tools as it was confined within the physical enterprise. When it comes to testing applications on the cloud, the choice of tools depends on the platform's ability to support the tool. It is also determined by the ability of the tool vendor to provide it in a pay-as-you-use mode. Testers need to understand that the fundamental virtue of cloud is to minimize the operating expenses of an on premise platform and derive cost efficiencies through sharing. The same holds true for the tools as well. While we can still have an on premise tool to test an application on the cloud, this would still be considered an overhead if the tool is used infrequently. Testers need to appreciate that cloud testing may require them to relearn how to use tools that are specifically designed to support an *on-demand* mode, as offered by vendors and supported by the cloud. Refer to the following diagram:

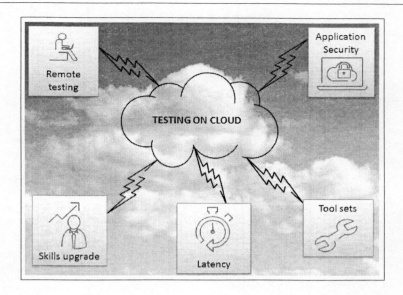

Conclusion

Shattering the delusion: Applications hosted on the cloud present a unique set of challenges that a tester needs to address. Test teams tasked with the responsibility of quality assurance must ensure that the same level of secure service is delivered by the applications with no degradation of experience to end users. To achieve this goal, testers need to understand the foundation, building blocks, and limitations of cloud architecture. This involves a radical change in the way testers think today and includes utilizing the following skills:

- An ability to accept the unseen
- An understanding that security is integral to testing
- The acceptance of remote testing as a new norm
- A willingness to equip themselves with new toolsets and skills

The cloud is here to stay, and its use will only increase over time. This is because it provides advantages far greater than its on premise counterpart. These include technologically superior hosting platforms, guaranteed cost savings, robust security features, and almost infinite scalability. It's time that we as testers prepare ourselves to master and test this inevitable technological asset that is invisible, yet omnipresent.

26

On-Demand Performance Testing on Self-Service Environments

Today, more and more companies are joining the bandwagon of embracing cloud strategies fueled by digital and DevOps initiatives to achieve agility and cost reduction. This has triggered the need for the right strategy to drive security and performance testing on cloud. The importance of testing strategy in the context of Digital and DevOps on cloud has assumed importance as well.

The digital-savvy organizations are leveraging on-demand, ready-to-use test environments to drive the capital expense intensive performance testing. The need to cut costs and reduce the cycle time is driving the organizations to conduct performance tests on the on-demand cloud-based environments. This, in turn, is opening up opportunities for end-to-end on-demand testing platforms packaged to drive mobile testing, performance testing, and SaaS testing activities.

In this chapter, we will discuss the following topics:

- Key challenges in on-demand performance testing
- Proposed solution (**performance testing as a service – PTaaS**)
- Key solution components of PTaaS

On-demand performance testing environments — key challenges and solutions

The idea of on-demand performance testing environment is a compelling one, but it requires managing queries on data security and the environment setup, which could be an accurate representation of production.

To address data security, we need to generate synthetic data/scrub production data to create test data for performance testing. The **Test Data Management (TDM)** tools, such as Datamaker from CA, help to generate synthetic data based on the database profiles and configuration.

Production-like environments can be created on cloud manually or using tools such as Skytap. In handling this manually, one goes about gathering the required production configuration data. The tools, such as Skytap, do the same by reading the production environment configuration from the customer production data center and recreate the environment on the cloud. The automation tool helps maintain the accuracy of the production-like environment since manual efforts are minimized. Hence, the automation tool enhances the quality of the test results.

Need for a cloud platform to build end-to-end performance testing

Environment availability of ready-to-use cloud infrastructures along with the required tooling is important to build end-to-end performance testing environment. The cloud environment supports the provisioning of the required infrastructure with a choice of configuration, testing tools, reports, and operational support. Many organizations have cloud and provisioning of environments on public and private clouds.

The typical components of a cloud platform include the following:

- Provisioning a development and test environment on cloud
- A portal for development and test teams to track the status and usage of environments and offer them self-service
- Use of environment templates for quick provisioning of environments
- Run processes to provide operations support to the development and test teams
- On-demand provisioning of tools (for example, HPE Loadrunner)

On-demand self-service environments for carrying out performance testing

PTaaS solutions can offer on-demand performance testing for self-service environments. PTaaS can offer end-to-end performance testing and engineering, from test strategy and planning, scripting, and test execution to analysis and recommendations.

A typical PTaaS solution has the following features:

- Provisioning of infrastructure, testing and engineering tools, and resources on-demand
- Infrastructure, application, tool, and resource support
- Built-in TDM tools for test cata creation addressing the security aspects
- Test environment management
- Capabilities to virtually provision the dependent applications and third-party interfaces

Typical benefits of a PTaaS solution include the following things:

- Scalability of infrastructure on-demand
- No up-front capital investment required
- On-demand infrastructure available on a consumption-based model
- Substantial savings on performance testing cost

Key scenarios for on-demand performance testing – proposed architecture

The requirements for conducting a performance test outside the customer data center can be categorized under the following use cases:

- **Scenario-1**: Applications, environments, and performance testing tools on the same cloud
- **Scenario-2**: Applications, environments, and performance testing tools on disparate clouds

We will now discuss these scenarios and the proposed architecture.

Scenario-1 — Architecture and how performance testing is carried out

The following diagram depicts the use case-1 scenario:

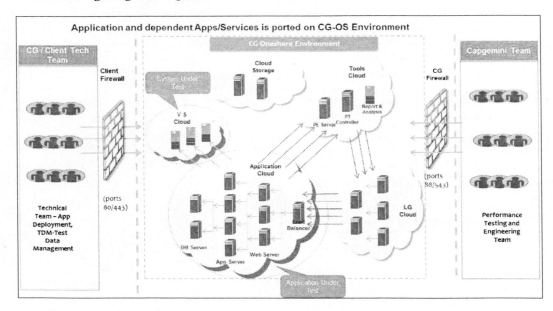

We will get to learn the following things from the preceding screenshot:

- Complete applications, dependent apps/services, third-party applications, and PT and E tools are ported on a single cloud environment

- Applications are deployed on cloud, including load balancers, web server, app server, and database server

- Dependent application or third-party application virtualization

- Tool servers are deployed on the cloud, such as HP LR Controller, Dynatrace EM, and reporting and analysis

- Load testing tool load generators deployed on the cloud for generating load on the application teams involved:

  ◦ The provider and client project team — technical architect, development team, test data management team

  ◦ The testing provider team to perform SIT, regression test, performance test, security test, and so on

Scenario-2 — Architecture and how performance testing is carried out

The cloud-cloud communication is enabled by tools (like MuleSoft).

The following diagram depicts the use case-2 scenario:

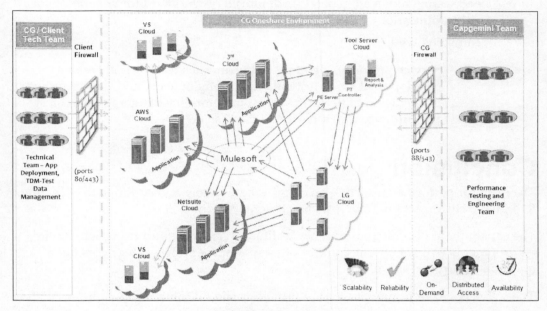

Multi-Cloud Environment

PTaaS is the proposed solution addressing the performance testing on-demand on cloud enabled by HP tools available on Microsoft Azure cloud platform and a service provider handling customer requirements. Let's see the things that help us here:

- Complete application, performance testing and engineering tools, dependent applications/services, and third-party applications are deployed on multi-cloud environment and integration platform such as MuleSoft software used for integrating all the applications

- Application, web server, app server, database server, and third-party application deployed on cloud

- Application, web server, app server, database server, and third-party application deployed on AWS cloud

- Application, web server, app server, database server, and third-party application deployed on Netsuite cloud

- Integration platform for connecting applications, data sources, and APIs in the cloud or on premises

- Dependent application or third-party application virtualization

- Tool server deployed on the cloud, such as HPE Loadrunner Controller, Dynatrace environment management, and reporting and analysis

- Load testing tool load generators deployed on the cloud for generating load on the application

- Teams involved:

  - Service provider/client project team, such as technical architect, development team, test data management team, and service provider testing team to perform system integration testing, regression test, performance test, security test, and so on

Conclusion

The need for performance testing on cloud is here to stay and continue to grow due to digital transformation, DevOps, and cloud adoption.

The capability to provide performance testing services on cloud using self-service environments will not only become a differentiator for system integrators but a question of survival as well.

The self-service environments service providers should think through differentiating their offering by including more choice of testing tools (COTS and open source), test data management, customer environment cloning capabilities, DevOps support, reporting, security, and ease of use.

Performance testing can be complex and time consuming and requires expert time, expensive tools, and resources. PTaaS allows organizations to pay based on consumption, reducing the capital investment and risk for the client besides, cutting down on testing cycle time and time to market.

27
Quality Assurance for Digital Marketing Initiatives

Organizations across the world are rapidly digitizing their businesses today as they face intense pressure to transform their businesses to stay competitive. The marketing function is dominated by the influence of social media technologies.

Digitizing or transforming toward digital indicates that organizations will do the following things:

- Leverage analytics at both the predictive and reactive stages to understand their customers' buying behavioral patterns
- Go mobile in the smartphone dominated marketplace
- Engage with their customers through social media
- Leverage the use of connected devices

Evolution of digital marketing

The digital paradigm comprises of areas such as digital marketing, digital customer management, and business process management. However, digital media is so pervasive that customers want to access information at their fingertips, on the go. Customers have brand preferences and like to receive personalized communication about shopping events and brand offers tailored to our needs. This is precisely why organizations need to understand how their customers behave on social media, and it is one of the reasons for digital marketing to take predominance in the industry over other digitization initiatives that organizations adopt today.

Three features are require to characterized the digital transformation:

Characteristics of Digital Transformation		Customer Centricity	Increased Velocity and Agility	Adapt to new technologies

Digital marketing is the practice of promoting products and services using digital platforms and distribution channels. In order to assure the organizations of the fact that the objectives behind the IT implementation of digital marketing have been successful, it is imperative that we *test* the software behind the business strategy well.

Challenges of implementing digital marketing

The challenges of implementing digital marketing include the following ones:

- Varied and rapidly changing technological base demanding more agility in application deployments.

- High volumes demand that not only should the technology deployed be functionally scalable, but should also be capable of retaining consumer attention by ensuring that frontend channels are well designed for ease of use. For example, by functional scalability, we mean that a customer should be able to navigate all the products and services that the organization offers on a single platform. Ease of use refers to customer experience and easy to carry out end-to-end transactions.

- Ensuring information security in digital marketing is exposed to the most vulnerabilities as the organizations' applications get exposed to a larger public through websites, portals, shopping carts, and so on.

Need for quality focus in digital marketing initiatives

While ensuring comprehensive quality checks on content and messages that remain the backbone of marketing, their broadcast on omni-channels across regions, leveraging social media, partner portals, and mobile devices through search engines have added complexities around validating interface and integration validation.

In addition to complying with performance and availability SLAs, compliance to organizational, regional, and partner policies is of utmost importance. Taking this into consideration marketers (CMOs) have to ensure that a comprehensive QA policy is in place, taking care of with holistic validation to ensure quality focus.

The demands of competitive leadership and shrinking timelines have raised the expectations of having customer-centric quality content and message. Comprehensive quality checks on marketing artifacts have gained renewed focus with providers building QA solutions specific to digital marketing.

QA of digital marketing applications – key validations

QA of digital marketing applications should include validation of content quality, message quality, and social media:

Content	Messaging	Social Media
Usability	User Experience	Views
Readiness	Digital Persuasion	Time
Compliance	Predictability	Conversations
Statutory	Performance	Clicks
Organizational	Uniformity	Product time
Relevancy	Window Resize Impact	Platform Integration
Compelling Graphics	Email Actions	3rd party Integration
Keywords & Keyword Ranking	Open	Follower Growth
Availability on partner platforms	Actioned	Click-Through rate
Hyper Links-Hot, Cold, Broken	Delete	Publishing Volume
Printer Friendly Versions	Banner Ads	Average Interaction per
Rules	Clicks	post
Segmentation & Situations	Amplification Rates	Drop Off rate
Security	Bounce Rates	Media Tone
Native Advertising	Subscribe / Unsubscribe Rate	

Analytics		
Product / Page Views & Time	Data Flow	Traffic Analysis
Product / Page Time	Relevancy	Surveys
Customer Acquisition & Retention	Behavioral	Market Reach
Customer Monetization	Data Acquisition & Distribution	Clicks
Visits-How Often / Soon	Report Structure & Content	Proliferations
Data Integration & Integrity ETL	Reject Condition Validation	Market Penetration
	Data Quality	Data Stores

We will see all the preceding things in more detail in the following list:

- **Content quality validation**: This involves the testing of the content displayed to prospective consumers for characteristics such as usability, high availability, compliance to standards, and compelling graphics. The content needs to be tested for accessibility of the links/hyperlinks that need to direct to the appropriate web page. Countries such as the USA and Europe have mandated accessibility according to the WCAG guidelines.

- **Message quality validation**: This ensures that the messages displayed on the website are tested for uniformity, multi-browser and mutli-channel compatibility, and visual and voice compatibility.

- **Social media integration and interface validation**: This involves the testing of content for integration and interface with various social media channels (for example, a company's home page or sales promotion web page being invoked from Facebook), security, user experience, and compliance to the standards such as PCI DSS.

- **Data and report quality validation**: In today's world, when most decisions are based on data, not having an accurate data quality plan, the right analytics algorithm, and dashboard can only result in chaos, adding to the effort where marketers are trying to get their heads around creating and broadcasting customer-centric content. This could put the entire exercise of the digital marketing program in jeopardy to the extent of it being called off.

A comprehensive end-to-end QA and improvement plan around **Performance, User Experience, Security, Functionality**, and **Interoperability** leads to more control over the business outcome and faster time to deployment (automated validations), and its implementation is the only answer to de-risk the digital marketing campaigns. In the absence of this, the following illustration can hold true:

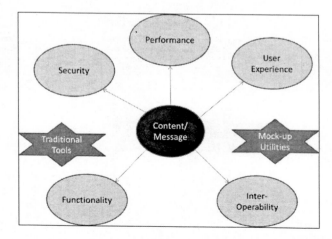

Conclusion

Working in the innovative digital era is powered by technology and driven by speed. At the same time, end clients must be addressed *First Time Right*. Ensuring high quality technology through structured testing is not enough, clients expect more and want the testing and quality assurance discipline to significantly contribute to their business goals, secure and improve the corporate image, and improve sales through digital marketing campaigns. The testing and QA profession now has the opportunity to pick up the challenge and transform to the role of a business value assurance provider.

28

Security Dashboard for the Board

The topic of cybersecurity did not fetch boardroom attention until recently; metrics and dashboards remained the subject matter of QA professionals. There is growing importance of cybersecurity in today's world where more and more business is conducted online. Board members are nowadays interested to reduce business risk and cyber-security risk is certainly the topmost risk in today's businesses.

In this chapter, we will discuss the following topics:

- Need for monitoring and reporting security threats
- Parameters to be monitored and reported
- Metrics-based reporting and an illustrative dashboard
- The consequences of security lapses
- Challenges in implementing a dashboard

Why security threats need to be monitored and reported?

All systems are prone to vulnerabilities that can be exploited by malicious software and agents. Developers and users of IT need to assess and manage the risk from unavoidable security vulnerabilities and threats. One of the biggest challenges is to identify and measure relevant security parameters for supporting decision-making. Capgemini Cybersecurity survey sheds light on the risks that organizations are facing. Take a look at the following image:

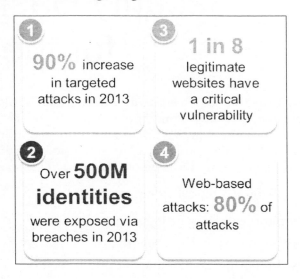

The determination of security parameters and their quantification can't be a trivial matter. On one hand, the parameters need to be applicable to the low-level components and, on the other, the same parameter should be usable for very different purposes such as compliance with standards, contractual requirements, comparison with benchmarking, and so on.

What should be monitored and reported?

Both the internal and external use of security parameters require evidence and should help in stating the quantification of security factors. One needs to ensure the right terminology of security parameters. Listed are some of the key parameters around which security metrics need to be captured. It will be valuable to ensure that parameters capture two main dimensions: the severity and impact of the incidence.

Application security/vulnerability management

Application security encompasses measures throughout the code's life cycle to prevent gaps in the security policy of an application or the underlying system (vulnerabilities) through flaws in the design, development, deployment, upgrade, or maintenance of the application.

- **Vulnerability**: A weakness of the (sub)system, which can be exploited for impairing its services or affecting its assets

- **Threat**: A potential for violation of security, which exists when there is an action or event that could breach security and cause harm

- **Attack**: Identified as a process implemented by a threat agent to exploit a system by taking advantage of one or more vulnerabilities

- **Countermeasure**: It is a set of actions to avoid/mitigate undesired malicious actions against a system

Many of the vulnerabilities can be discovered with a vulnerability scanner, which searches for open ports, insecure software configuration and susceptibility to malware, buffer overflow, and similar things. In addition, antivirus software capable of heuristic can help discover undocumented malware (for example, a software attempting to overwrite a system file). In addition, penetration tests should be performed to uncover the vulnerabilities left undetected even after vulnerability scans.

Correcting vulnerabilities may involve the installation of a patch, a change in network security policy, reconfiguration of software (such as a firewall), educating users about social engineering, or incident management.

Before we discuss how to address vulnerabilities, a word of caution is important. Addressing vulnerabilities through patches, configuration management, and so on, methods later in life cycle once the software is released is exorbitantly expensive. It is always advisable to address vulnerabilities early in the life cycle—during the requirement analysis, design, and development phases.

Let's discuss these methods.

- **Patch Management**: It involves acquiring, testing, and installing multiple patches (code changes) to a system. Patch management activities include the following ones:
  - Maintaining current knowledge of the available patches
  - Deciding what patches are appropriate for particular systems
  - Ensuring that patches are installed properly
  - Testing systems after installation
  - Documenting all associated procedures, such as specific configurations

- **Configuration Change Management**: It is a process for establishing and maintaining the consistency of a product's performance, functional, and physical attributes with its requirements, design, and operational information throughout its life.

- **Incident Management**: It identifies, analyzes, and corrects hazards to prevent a future reoccurrence. Such incidents within an organization are dealt with by an **Incident Response Team (IRT)/Incident Management Team (IMT)**.

Specific metrics to be reported in dashboard

To ensure that security monitoring and reporting is carried out objectively, there is a need for dashboard to be periodically presented and reviewed. A typical security dashboard should cover key metrics pertaining to business and financial, risk coverage, vulnerability, patch, incident, and change management.

Financial/business metrics include the following things:

- Information security budget as % of IT budget
- Financial losses (direct and indirect) caused by security breaches
- Impact of damage to reputation and trust
- Cost of (loss due to) data breaches, exposed user credentials, information leakage, and so on
- Impact of business disruptions caused by security incidents

Risk and security coverage includes the given things:

- Risk assessment coverage (% covered against overall applications and against critical applications)
- Security testing coverage (% covered against overall applications and against critical applications)

Vulnerability management includes the mentioned ones:

- Vulnerability scan coverage
- % of systems without known severe vulnerabilities
- Mean-time to mitigate vulnerabilities
- Number of known vulnerability instances

Patch management includes the listed things:

- Patch policy compliance
- Patch management coverage
- Mean-time to patch

Configuration change management includes the following things:

- Mean-time to complete changes
- % of changes with security review
- % of changes with security exceptions

Incident management includes the given things:

- Mean-time to incident discovery
- Incident rate
- Mean-time between security incidents
- Mean-time to recovery
- % of incidents detected by internal controls

Consequences of security lapses

Is it enough if the earlier metrics are regularly reported and monitored? A good dashboard can only provide a good starting point to deep-dive further and investigate more.

The consequences of security lapses, inability to monitor and report on the same include losses including direct/indirect financial loss, loss to reputation, business disruptions, and data breach loss:

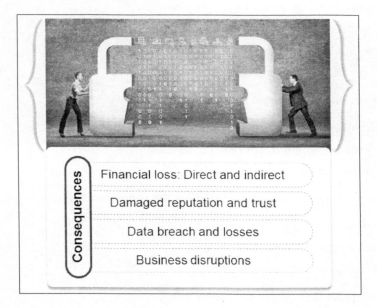

Consequences
- Financial loss: Direct and indirect
- Damaged reputation and trust
- Data breach and losses
- Business disruptions

Key challenges in implementing a dashboard

The key challenges in implementing a good metrics and dashboard program include the following things:

- Difficulty in estimating cost of data breaches
- Difficulty in detecting unknown malwares
- Difficulty in identifying a new vulnerability
- Difficulty in ensuring controls during systems development
- Difficulty in getting attention for information security as a formal program at the organization level

Conclusion

Dashboards can help, but not replace the need for foresight. Security dashboards are critical for the board to review regularly and act upon to save their organizations from cyber threats.

Key focus of the board members is to monitor financial/business metrics to avoid financial losses, reduce damage to reputation and trust, avoid the cost of data breaches, and eliminate business disruptions. Unfortunately, these metrics are not always easy to compute as no one wants to allocate budget thinking of potential incidents and losses.

29

Applying Robotic Automation to Mobile Applications Testing

Software robotics is simply automation or automation with human-like skill. Bots can't make judgments, and they only handle structured, rule-based processes that can be moved offline for backend execution. The bots don't, for example, interact with the customer who needs a SIM card activated. The customer service representative, though, can enter the customer details and push the activation process work to a software robot for processing. It is estimated that 15 minutes of human work can be handled in 1 minute by a bot.

In this chapter, we will cover the following topics:

- Software robots and key areas of their applicability
- Benefits of Robotic Process Automation (RPA)
- An example of implementing RPA for mobile testing and the tools involved

Software robot and their applicability

The applicability of software robots is in the following areas:

- **Process Automation**: The process automation can be deployed both in IT and clerical back-office work that involves a rule-based, non-subjective process without compromising the existing IT architecture. In the Business Process, the potential tasks for automation could be back-office tasks in finance, procurement, supply chain management, accounting, customer service, and human resources, including data entry, purchase order issuing, and creation of online access credentials.

- **IT support and management**: Automated processes in the remote management of IT infrastructures can investigate and solve problems for a faster process throughout. The software support Robots can improve service desk operations and the monitoring of network devices.

- **Software Test Automation**: Any manual testing activities that are data and rules driven can be supplemented with Robotic automation solution. This can be applied to areas of testing, such as UI test automation, mobile testing on devices/platforms, GUI automation, and content validation.

The benefits of Robotic Process Automation (RPA)

The benefits of **Robotic Process Automation (RPA)** include the following ones:

- **Lower cost**: Robots work 24/7/365 and deliver 25-50 % cost savings depending on the complexity of work as compared to human-based cost

- **Higher efficiency**: Robots deliver the rule-based work with zero errors and with reduced cycle time

- **Greater performance and quality**: Robots can perform redundant tasks tirelessly with better quality and output

- **Built Capacity**: Robots can scale and help in building capacity within the organization

Implementing RPA for mobile testing

Mobile testing challenges include the given ones:

- Testing across browsers

- Fragmentation caused by multiple varieties of handsets with different OS versions

- Increased frequency of newer OS versions and patch releases

- Heterogeneity based on screen size, OEM, operators, and so on

- Unavailability of the required device when needed

- Unavailability of all required devices in in-house or service provider labs, such as device anywhere

- Identifying an optimal combination of the required devices/OSes/browsers to optimize the testing efforts

- Variety of Mobile Application categories — Native, Web, and Hybrid

Take a look at the following block diagram:

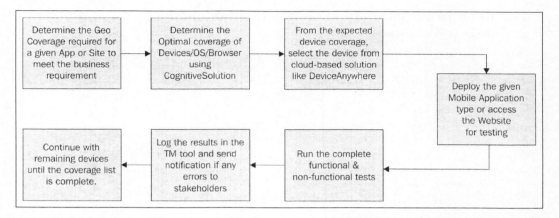

Let's discuss how these challenges are addressed by applying RPA:

- **Optimizing the device coverage**: *Are We Testing On the Right Devices and Platforms?*, is the question often application developers, testers, and product managers ask. The optimal coverage of devices/OSes/browsers for a given application type or site can be derived with multiple methods, such as the following ones:

  ° Profile data from Google analytics

  ° Using a sophisticated cognitive solution, such as IBM Watson

- **Device selection based on the required coverage**: Cloud-based solution supported by tools like **DeviceAnywhere** should be used to run the test. These tools ensure the quality of mobile applications and Websites by testing on real devices — smart phones, tablets, and other live carrier networks around the world.

The repetitive steps to select the real devices from emulators, such as DeviceAnywhere, can be recorded using tools like UiPath the Process robots can be created. The Process robot can select the device, deploy the application, and invoke the Test Robots to perform functional testing. This process is repeated until all the devices are exhausted from the device coverage list.

The steps to use cloud solutions, such as DeviceAnywhere, are as follows:

1. Launch a web browser and navigate to device anywhere URL [1], as shown in the following screenshot:

2. Click on **Login** in the top-right corner to log in:

3. After logging in, the user can navigate to **Test Centre**.

User can view all the devices and interact with them.

From the Device list, a user can acquire devices and run the required test.

A user can retrieve the Applications and deploy for testing or access the Mobile site for testing.

The image of the Application or Mobile can be compared using cognitive solution to ensure that the correct Application or site is being tested:

Mobile Application Testing using Test Robots — the robotic activities for application selection and testing include the following ones:

- **Process robots**: This helps in the selection of the device/platform from the coverage list, deploying the App from the App store, or accessing the given Micro site from Internet for testing.
- **Test Robots**: This helps in executing the function tests.

The Process robot and Test Robot work in tandem until the testing for all the devices from the coverage list is completed.

The steps to create Process and Test Robot using tools, such as UIPath, include the illustrated ones:

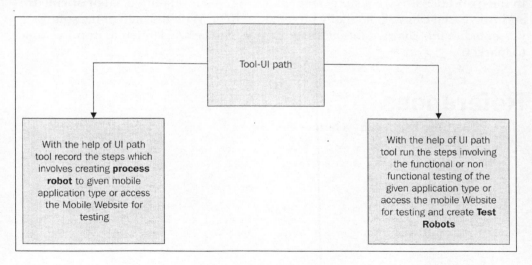

The proposed Robots can record and run task for multiple devices:

- Robots allows smooth collaboration between Tester and Robots.
- Tester guides the Process robot on the steps to select devices from cloud solution and deploy given application type or Mobile website. Process robot records all the steps.
- Test Robot runs the test steps based on the recording from UIPath, validates functional and non-functional features, and updates the results to the Test Management tool and sends notifications in case of any error.
- In case of any exception, Test Robot can transfer them to tester to handle.

The preceding steps of record and run from Process robot and Test robot respectively can continue until the device coverage list is complete.

Hence, activities' end-to-end process is totally outsourced to robots. All manual intensive, repetitive, and few judgment-based decisions can be carried out by robots. Robots connect the existing tools and humans handle only exceptions.

Conclusion

In the world of software testing, manual testing that is repetitive, labor oriented, and rule-based can be potentially targeted for RPA. With the help of the solutions presented in this chapter, mobile testing cycles can be accelerated to improve time to market.

References

- **Keynote Deviceanywhere** — www.keynote.com/solutions/testing/mobile-testing

30

Key Considerations in Testing Internet of Things (IoT) Applications

The **Internet of Things (IoT)** is an environment in which objects, animals, or people are provided with unique identifiers and the ability to transfer data over a network without requiring human-to-human or human-to-computer interaction.

This enables them to share intelligent information with each other or to the backend database directly through embedded sensors and actuators connected over the Internet.

As per Gartner, by 2020, there will be over 26 billion connected devices; other research (Morgan Stanley, Hammersmith Group) predicts that it could be up to 100 billion. It means that there will be at least three times more IoT devices than the world population. Suffice it to say that the sheer number of IoT devices is going to be mind-boggling in the near future.

In this chapter, we will discuss:

- Need for a robust IoT test strategy
- IoT revolution—trends
- IoT testing considerations
- Types of testing to be carried out

Refer to the following image:

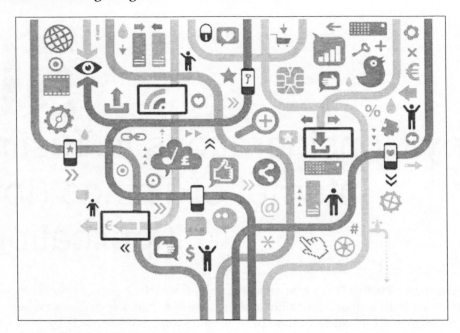

Need for a robust IoT test strategy

IOT technology, in the form of digital disruption, has entered the enterprise space at such a pace that companies do not have robust enough strategies to rigorously test the related hardware and software. Moreover, the huge volume of data getting captured and sent through IOT devices to the backend makes the system prone to performance bottlenecks.

An example could be your fitbit health device that captures your daily activity, food, and other health goals that you set up. Two key areas (among many others) that you would surely be concerned with are:

- Whether it captures the body movements accurately to count activity and calories consumed through the activity

- The performance of application when you synchronize the device with the application on server, especially considering that thousands of other users might be concurrently synchronizing their devices

As companies are pulling in technology from different sources, it becomes even more difficult to build a comprehensive testing strategy that can be easily implemented.

IoT Revolution – key findings from the World Quality Report 2016

As per the WQR2016, 85% of respondents have IoT as part of their business, but 68% do not have test strategy for IOT. Refer to the following graph:

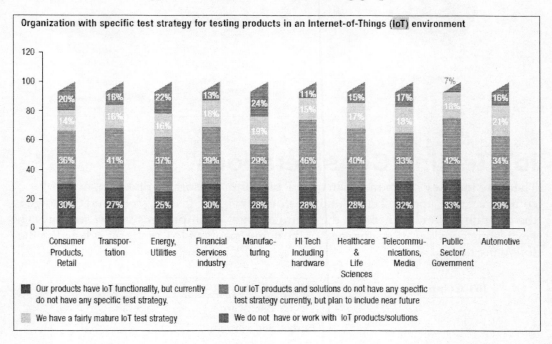

As per the WQR 2016, key opportunities for solutions for IoT include:

- Operational Intelligence
- Virtualization of services and APIs
- Tools for stress testing IoT middleware and gateways
- Creating protocols and device simulators

The following diagram explains the opportunities for IoT testing:

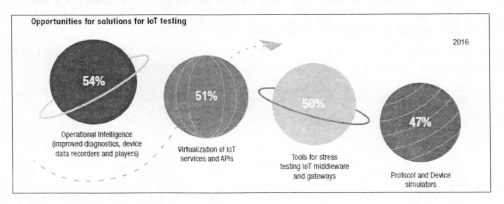

IoT Testing Considerations

There are four key components in an IoT platform: sensors, application, network communication, and backend database. Identifying the testing scope and coverage is the most important element for the formulation of a comprehensive test strategy. The key testing considerations for each of the components of IoT platform is listed in the following table:

IoT Component	What to Test
Sensors	Device hardware
	Embedded software
	Sensor response time and performance
	Error handling mechanism
Application	Application functionality
	User friendliness
	User roles and access levels
	Multiple request handling
Network Communication	Network connectivity
	Interaction between devices
	Data transmission frequency
Backend Database	Data packets for data losses
	Data encryption/decryption
	Data consistency and integrity validation
	Verification of data values

IoT testing types

With data being acquired from disparate sources (machines, inventory, equipment, tools, products, people, sensors, production logs, and so on.) over IoT platforms, quality assurance around functionality, scalability, compatibility, reliability, usability, security, speed, and integrity will ensure accurate and timely outcomes. The following testing types can be considered for IoT, depending on various testing considerations:

- **Functional testing**: Testing the functionality of the software application in order to validate the user stories and requirements.

- **Scalability testing**: Validating the ability of the I0T platform to support multiple concurrent users without degrading the performance.

- **Compatibility testing**: Validating the possible working combination of device hardware, communication protocol versions, software versions, and operating systems.

- **Reliability testing**: Validating IoT components (especially sensors) in various environmental and operational conditions.

- **Usability testing**: Ensuring the best-in-class user experience through visual appeal of text and content, user friendliness of the application, availability of useful information, error handling, and so on.

- **Security testing**: Identifying and eliminating vulnerabilities by validating the user roles and access levels, data privacy and data encryption methodologies, network security standards, and so on.

- **Network testing**: Testing the IoT application in various network connections and connection protocols to ensure seamless connectivity across the IoT platform.

- **Database testing**: Testing the backend database for the data types and values, data integrity, and data consistency.

- **Performance testing**: Validating that the response time of the sensors and the application is within the specified limit. Also, validating the performance of data reading, writing, and data retrieval rate is one of the key aspects of performance testing in IoT.

Conclusion

IoT technology is finding its applications in all the business sectors and it is increasingly going to be a permanent element of day-to-day life. Testing in IoT platforms is going to require a combination of various types of testing, depending on the domain and actual field of application. The IoT testing strategy will have the flavor of embedded testing and application testing, and moreover, it will span most of the functional and non-functional testing types based on the testing focus. There can be guidelines for formulating the overall IoT test strategy; however, it needs to be tweaked and testing types need to be refocused and defocused based on the actual field of application.

References

- `www.worldqualityreport.com`: Capgemini Sogeti HPE World Quality Report 2016

31

Algorithmic Business – In Need of Model-Based Testing

"The Goal is to turn data into information, and information into insights"

-Carly Fiorina (Ex-CEO HP)

An intriguing quote, isn't it? These words touch on one of the most important elements of data collection. Earlier, **big data** had become a buzzword; industry leaders had to recognize that value didn't lie uniquely in the quantity, but rather in the quality, insights, and analysis these numbers could provide.

The power of information has created many businesses. There are businesses that thrive on the use of algorithms. In this chapter, we will discuss the following topics:

- An introduction to algorithmic business
- The journey of analytics in algorithmic businesses
- An illustration of algorithmic business
- The implication for testing in an algorithmic business
- The use of model-based testing in algorithmic businesses

Introduction and journey of analytics

Algorithmic business, an advanced version of analytics, has emerged as the next big thing. Analytics strengthen an organization's understanding of the customers' needs, likes, and dislikes. To fuel these studies, organizations are collecting data from numerous physical and virtual sensors through initiatives, such as digital transformation and **Internet of Things (IoT)**. The collected data then is analyzed in order to generate meaningful insights for companies. This paradigm shift has affected the entire market. **WQR2016** illustrates how companies are embracing both digital transformation and IoT as tools to analyze and engage with customers in an efficient way, having a strong impact on the processes, procedures, and tools adopted by the IT industry:

In short, data can be amassed from various physical and virtual sources. Processing this data requires a step-by-step process that provides valuable insight at every level. Each stage's data offers new information that helps companies to make strategic decisions.

The first step shown in the preceding diagram, known as **Big Data**, comprises a collection of raw data, not ideal for human interpretation. This raw data, when summarized in a certain way (number of counts, likes, average, sum, and so on), generates meaningful information for interpretation. The next stage is called **Descriptive Analytics,** and some of the examples include social media likes, financial reports, and inventory details. With the third step, known as **Predictive Analytics**, we can further process data and probable outcomes using both data modeling and machine learning techniques. When applied, these analytics can generate sales forecasts for the next year and calculate the probability of customers making future credit payments on time. Companies are designing applications and business models that can respond quickly to customer needs and apply automation to ensure timely response. Furthermore, various algorithms are being embedded in business applications that make relevant decisions in the last stage known as **Prescriptive Analytics**. These types of models are equipped with a feedback loop and a system linked to a particular algorithm that responds to end users automatically. Businesses adopting this algorithmic approach are called **algorithmic businesses**.

Algorithmic business – an illustration

As Gartner explained, *Algorithmic business involves the industrialized use of complex mathematical algorithms pivotal to driving improved business decisions or process automation for competitive differentiation.*

The building blocks of any system following algorithmic business logic contain **input**, **output**, and a **feedback loop**. Input, a system using Decision tree, Fuzzy logic, Excel, SAS, SAP, Tibco Software, MathWorks, or Ayata is analyzed by an algorithmic function driven by the feedback loop and based on the analysis the output function provides. Depending on the output system, the application changes the resulting output in forms, such as price, inventory details, patient's statistics, and others. The following model shows a high-level understanding of the algorithmic business approach:

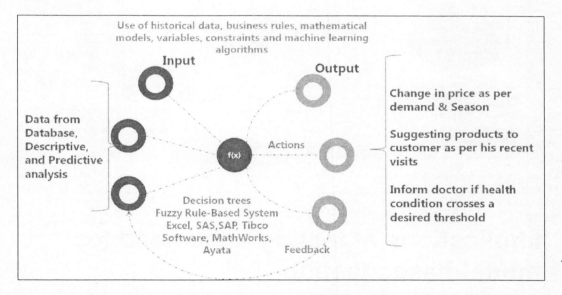

To better illustrate this practice, let's take the example of Amazon.com. Amazon has a recommendation engine that gives suggestions to online buyers about products they may have they viewed, purchased, or kept in their virtual cart. This engine is very dynamic, and changes the suggestions based on the customer's recent searches and purchases. Amazon once reported that this approach helped them to increase sales by 29%. Many other industries are using an algorithmic approach to better target their customers. The following image provides a snapshot of few other industries using this approach:

Recruitment	Transportation	Health Care

Use of IBM's Watson & IBM Biginsights for employee recruitment, internal mobility, and career development	Take Example of Cab and airline services	Take Example of Hospital in Modern world
Matching Resume in database, Social media w.r.t skills	Use of algorithmic approach to connect customer with driver near to him/her	Use of Descriptive, Predictive and Prescriptive Analytics to inform doctor about patient's health condition
Efficiencies in form of candidate relevancy, employee satisfaction and quick time to onboard	Use factors like seasonality, rush etc. to decide price of ticket	

Implications of testing – the need for model-based testing

In algorithmic-based applications, feedback loops continuously change inputs and outputs, limiting the use of standard testing techniques. Model-based testing techniques allow us to configure a desired business process through the use of tools, such as Conformiq, Reactis tester, TVG, and TorX. These model-based testing tools generate both test cases and test scripts automatically, autoexecute them, and analyze the test results. Every time feedback loop changes the input, model changes as required, and hence all test cases are changed automatically. Every time the feedback loop alters the input, the models change and the test cases are automatically updated. The most important part of model-based testing is designing a model for automated test case generation. This requires testers who are able to apply model-based thinking to test case generation based on the needs of an algorithmic business. Refer to the following diagram:

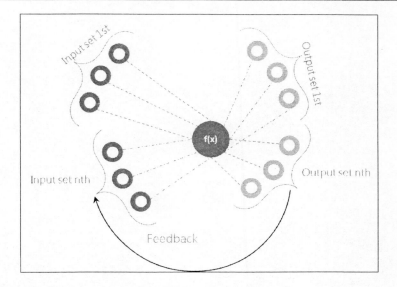

The benefits of model-based testing include the following:

- **Enabled dynamic testing**: Testing for algorithmic business involves multiple iterations of data in order to auto generate test cases and executions.

- **Improved time to market**: Automation is applied not only in test execution but also in test case generation.

- **Reuse potential**: Using models enables higher reuse for similar applications in algorithmic business.

Conclusion

Increased competition has forced businesses to innovate and to develop customer intimacy. The use of algorithms has helped businesses to study customer behavior and buying patterns in a dynamic digital business environment. Such businesses, known as algorithmic businesses, also need to apply models to their testing practice, as model-based testing tools and methodologies have helped reduce time to market and provide both cost and performance-related efficiencies.

32

Making Testing Adaptive, Interactive, Iterative, and Contextual with Cognitive Intelligence

Natural language and artificial intelligence areas of study have existed for nearly five decades. Now, these combined with predictive analytics have become the building blocks of cognitive analytics. Cognitive analytics systems are being utilized for computing with the goal of creating accurate models of how the human brain senses, reasons, and responds to a stimulus.

This chapter is about the use of cognitive intelligence in testing. In this chapter, we will discuss the following topics:

- An introduction to cognitive testing
- The evolution of cognitive technology and available platforms
- The methodologies involved
- It's advantages and some use cases
- The technologies supported
- The costs involved
- The challenges associated in Implementing

Background – cognitive intelligence

Nowadays, computers are improving with machine learning, and the use of products or solutions developed using latest technologies, such as data analytics, business intelligence, and big data. Computers can mimic the human brain and draw inferences from existing data and patterns with the help of underlying software. The software is also able to insert this back into its knowledge base for future inferences in the form a self-learning feedback loop. Cognitive intelligence makes a new class of problems computable. It addresses complex situations that are characterized by ambiguity and uncertainty that we can relate to humans.

What is cognitive testing all about?

Cognitive testing is a new class of testing and, as the name suggests, it leverages machine learning, artificial intelligence, natural language processing, and other cognitive computing techniques. I recently participated in a workshop in an effort to identify testing use cases that can benefit from IBM Watson's cognitive intelligence to testing and that led me to create an offering on cognitive testing. In this section, I will cover the evolution of cognitive technology and available platforms, such as IBM Watson, methodologies involved in cognitive testing, benefits, technologies supported, sector-specific use cases, costs, and challenges in implementing.

Evolution of cognitive technology and available platforms

Cognitive computing is evolving, and the transformation is taking place from descriptive analytics to predictive analytics. The logical next step is to move toward prescriptive analytics to start taking decisions based on the analyzed information. This would create opportunities to create self-service testing platforms with self-healing capabilities. The advances in natural language processing would lead to more advanced scriptless testing solutions. Smart speech-to-text processing would enable the business users to narrate requirements in natural language orally and be able to convert them to automated test suites using scriptless testing techniques. Neuromorphic systems and neuro-enable firmware can be used for smart environment handling and intelligent test data management.

Some of the platforms available that offer cognitive intelligence are as follows:

- **OpenAI**: This is a nonprofit artificial intelligence research platform to benefit humanity, unconstrained by a need to generate financial return.

- **Google DeepMind**: This specializes in building algorithms that are capable of learning for themselves directly from raw experience or data and can perform across a wide variety of tasks.

- **IBM Watson**: This is a technology platform using natural language processing and machine learning that reveals insights from large amounts of unstructured data.

Methodologies involved in cognitive testing

Cognitive testing leverages machine learning, artificial intelligence, natural language processing, speech-to-text, image recognition, and similar cognitive computing techniques. Cognitive testing uses heuristics to predict defects and to measure system performance and optimize the test coverage based on assessed risk.

Products such as IBM Watson, Google Deepmind, and Microsoft Oxford provide platform for cognitive computing. The same can be leveraged for solving test optimization problems. Some examples of how cognitive intelligence can be leveraged in testing are as follows:

- Test prioritization

- Automated regression test bed selection and prioritization

- Failure prediction using log analyzers

- Test coverage optimization

- Comparing product module patterns in production vis-à-vis test coverage

- Bridging the gap in test coverage

- Determining how much testing is enough

- Assessing release readiness and provide a decision on halting regression

- Providing a risk index of product released to production

- Self-correcting/updating test suites

- Retiring the obsolete test cases and code fixes in the pipeline

- QA dashboard

- Reporting of metrics, such as cost of defect, resource utilization, and so on

Advantages of cognitive testing compared to the current methods

IBM Watson has been a pioneer in cognitive intelligence space. IBM Watson considers the four key advantages as Adaptive, Interactive, Iterative/Stateful, and Contextual.

The following are the advantages of cognitive systems in context of testing:

- **Adaptive**: Cognitive testing is adaptive, as it enables system to learn as information changes, and as goals and requirements evolve. For instance, based on the quality of code and changes in requirements, the system can suggest number of test iterations and decision on when to stop testing.

- **Interactive**: The system interacts easily with users so that the users can define their test requirements easily. They may also interact with other processors, IoT devices, and cloud services, as well as with people.

- **Iterative and stateful**: This feature helps the system remember previous interactions and returns suitable information for the specific application at a specific point in time. The testing sequence can be defined based on the questions asked.

- **Contextual**: This indicates the software is able to understand the context, for instance, meaning, time, location, appropriate domain, regulations, user's profile, process, task, and goal.

Sector specific use cases

Cognitive testing can be applied across industry sectors. However, its adoption has a linkage to the use of agile or DevOps software lifecycle. Highly competitive and new age industries are more likely to adopt cognitive solutions, whereas the more stable and highly regulated sectors are likely to prefer conventional testing solutions.

Telecom and financial services are the key users of cognitive intelligence. Healthcare can be another, but regulations may prevent machines making decisions for a patient's health. Financial services use cognitive systems in domains, such as **Know Your Customer (KYC)**, Credit Ratings and Loan decisions, and wealth management for portfolio optimization.

Technologies supported

The cognitive testing applies to all types of applications and is not just limited to web interfaces. The key principle behind cognitive testing is the ability of the system to access and analyze large volumes of data (both structured and unstructured). The system also applies machine learning to extract context sensitive intelligence from the analyzed data and use it to predict future behavior. All kinds of applications, for example, Cloud based, IoT, Mainframe, Database, Mobile, and so on, can benefit from cognitive testing techniques.

Consider an example of testing scenario: IBM Watson can crawl through the defect data, various requirements and design documents, development code base, and production incidents to identify likely points of failure. The intelligence gather can be used to tailor test execution plan accordingly. Platforms such as Watson (it all started out by Watson cracking the jeopardy show as an intelligent machine) have come a long way.

IBM Watson and other tools that form the basis of cognitive intelligence solutions can work on the code base as well. The tool can be configured to browse all leading technologies. There is a lot of intelligence that can be derived by analyzing the unstructured information embedded in the code comments. Also, the quality of the code base can be assessed by applying cognitive computing techniques to measure logical accuracy and to derive boundary conditions for test data preparation. The relative age of the underlying code, and the frequency of check-ins is also found to have a very strong co-relation with the defect density.

Costs involved

The methodology is expensive, but one does not need all the modules of a complex system such as Watson. An analysis is needed on the modules required, based on specific use cases, in case of perpetual enterprise licenses. To solve short-term problems, one can use the SaaS model at costs as low as US$30 to US$80 (€28 to €75) per-person-per-month based on features to be used. Enterprise use could come at costs ranging from US$1 to US$5 million (€0.9 to 4.7 million), including hardware costs.

Challenges associated in implementing cognitive technologies

The keys challenges in implementing cognitive testing include the following:

- **Need for training the system**: The system needs to be trained in the domain and application landscape, and this requires a significant investment in terms of time and effort during initial stages. However, there are great economies of scale once the system is trained, and the costs come down sharply.

- **Incorrect Requirements**: The cognitive computing system derives its intelligence from the requirements that are fed into the system. The challenges with incorrect requirements (lack of alignment with customer needs; ambiguous /inaccurate/invalid/infeasible requirements) could lead to incorrect test results.

- **Complex Architecture**: This challenge combined with the frequent technology and configuration changes pose technical challenges in implementing this technology.

Conclusion

Given the pressures of the industry, it's very obvious that the adoption of cognitive technologies is driven based on potential for increased revenue, lower costs, faster time-to-market, improved competitive positioning, and enhanced customer experience. Specifically related to testing, the benefits include fewer defects, improved test efficiencies, and a better collaboration between the development and testing teams.

FinTech – A New Disruptor in Industry and Implications for Testing and QA

FinTech, also known as Financial Technologies, hails from both technology and financial services. With digitization, new companies have evolved to provide customers online financial services. For this, companies have come up with software, frameworks, and solutions that allow customers to deal with their money online.

In this chapter, we will discuss:

- The FinTech ecosystem
- FinTech services and their impact on various sectors
- Testing considerations for FinTech solutions

FinTech ecosystem

A disruption in one industry triggers a cascading effect on the others.

The World FinTech Report 2017 explains that FinTech has emerged as one of the most promising trends of the recent past. Increasing customer expectations, the expansion of venture capital funding, reduced entry barriers, and technology innovations have allowed the FinTech Industry to flourish in every sector. The methods of offering services through traditional firms have not changed much over the years.

The fast-changing industry and busy schedules of individuals have highlighted many loopholes in traditional financial systems. On one hand, traditional financial firms believe that their business is at risk due to FinTech startups; on the other hand, various traditional firms are partnering with innovative FinTech firms to tap the market. The following image maps the FinTech ecosystem with financial service areas:

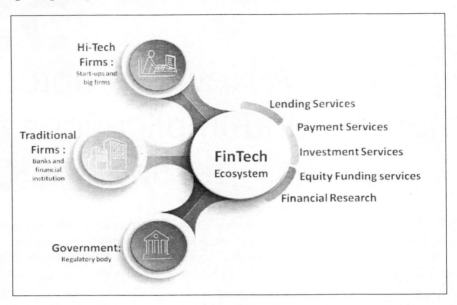

The FinTech ecosystem consists of three entities:

- **Hi-Tech Firms**: It consist of two kinds of companies: big technology companies like Apple and Google, who are becoming active in financial applications, and small companies like PayPal and Stripe, who are introducing disruptive technologies that enable clients to handle their money online.

- **Traditional Firms**: A second system, known as traditional firms, includes global and local banks and financial institutions. These traditional firms either partner with hi-tech firms or do in-house innovation to strengthen their market.

- **Government**: The third entity consists of a regulatory body, mainly government, which enforces regulations and policy settings. Services include payments, Blockchain transactions, wealth management, investment banking, retail banking, lending, and treasury functions.

FinTech services and their impact on various sectors

WQR2016 illustrates that financial firms are partnering with FinTech firms in order to make their presence known in the market. With the changing nature of firms, testing for related applications also changes. Today, we need agile delivery models, rapid QA and testing, and application programming interfaces with service virtualization. FinTech disruption has affected various sectors of the industry through its services, which are based on digital platforms. The following heat map shows the sectors with services currently having an immediate impact:

		Sectors						
		Banking & Insurance	Manufacturing	Health Care & Life Sciences	Consumer products and Retail	Technology Media & Entertainment	Telecom	Energy & Utilities
Services	Lending							
	Payment							
	Investment							
	Equity Funding							
	Short Term Credit							
	Financial Research							

Some of the FinTech services available include:

- **Lending services**: FinTech firms are offering peer-to-peer lending services, including online solutions that allow lenders and borrowers to work together. Borrowers, in this case, may be individuals or businesses. Examples include companies such as Lendbox and MarketFinance.

- **Payment services**: Companies are offering online payment solutions where buyers can pay online and the settlement of money can happen without going to a bank. Examples include companies such as Paytm and Mobikwik. This service has significantly altered the retail and e-commerce segments where customers use online channels or cards to pay.

- **Investment services**: A few start-ups are providing solutions that can give suggestions to people on their financial investments by comparing various policies within the market. Examples include companies such as PolicyBazaar and BankBazaar.

- **Equity funding services**: FinTech firms are using crowd-funding platforms to approach venture capital funding services. These services target start-ups and early-stage businesses. Examples include companies such as Ketto and Wishberry.

- **Short-term credit services**: This service has created a significant impact on the manufacturing industry. Solutions based on supply chain financing help buyers and suppliers to handle the whole retail process from procuring to paying. This service assists both parties to manage their working capital.

- **Financial research**: Fueled by analytics, some companies have innovated new solutions and tools that can analyze the financial condition of a firm or an economy. With the use of predictive analytics and business intelligence, companies such as Blue Yonder and Packetwerk are providing solutions for financial research.

Testing for FinTech applications or solutions

In order to test FinTech applications, we need to map out requirements and specific types of testing. For a FinTech application or software, there are five key requirements: security, data integrity, user friendliness, functionality, and performance. The following diagram illustrates each requirement in reference to testing:

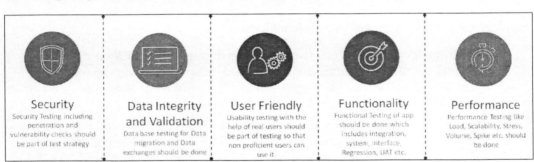

- Security is one of the most important aspects requiring testing in a FinTech application. Financial data used by applications contains sensitive information that can be misused by hackers and malicious software. As such, security testing, including penetration and vulnerability checks, is important.

- Data safety, data integrity, and data validation are important for any system, but are especially essential for financial systems. During data migration and data exchanges over communication channels, proper procedures and rules regarding tables and records must be followed.

- FinTech applications are used to expand both the reach and ease of business. Applications have to be user friendly so that any user is able operate it. Consequently, this requires usability testing with the help of real users.

- Furthermore, functional testing ought to be an integral part of test strategy, given that the applications interact with many other applications. Load and stress capabilities for applications should also be checked.

Conclusion

FinTech presents both threats and opportunities for traditional banking firms. This duality has resulted in a cascading effect on other sectors. Operational efficiency is one of the biggest achievements of FinTech, a technology that most traditional firms are lacking. Traditional firms have to demonstrate agility in building, acquiring, and partnering with FinTech firms in order to capitalize on market opportunities. Capgemini's world FinTech report suggests a methodical framework known as discover, devise, deploy, and sustain. With the help of senior leadership commitment and a clear vision, this framework can help traditional firms to compete through the use of this disruption.

34

Blockchain Technology – Assuring Secure Business

"The blockchain is the most important technology since the Internet itself"

-Marc Andreessen

Since the advent of the Internet, security has been a concern to organizations and individuals. Most organizations, especially in financial services, fear to store their documents and monetary information on the Internet. Individuals hesitate transacting online due to hacking and other security problems. Blockchain technology has evolved recently to solve this problem.

In this chapter, we will discuss:

- Blockchains and the process involved
- Some popular types of blockchains
- Testing considerations

Introduction to blockchain

A blockchain is a type of data structure where information can be stored with some additional information for validations. This technology records every transaction like a ledger and checks its authenticity/relevancy by validating it with previous transactions. These blocks or pieces of information are copied on every node or system in the network, and hence it is called a distributed ledger.

We can define a blockchain as — *a distributed cryptographic ledger that enables transactions via digital validation.*

The blockchain process

The whole process can be understood in three simple steps:

- Request for transaction
- Validation of information
- Addition of a new block

Refer to the following image for a clearer understanding of the blockchain process:

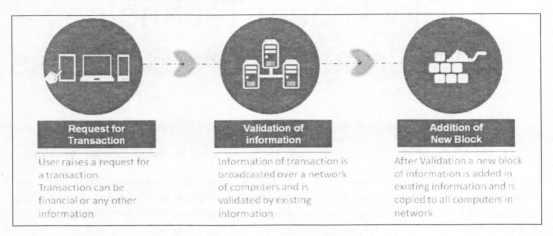

The blockchain process starts with a **request** from a user who wants to do a transaction. This transaction can be cryptocurrency, records, or any other information. The information is broadcasted over a network of many computers. These computers are called **nodes**. These nodes contain information about the existing blockchain of information. Using algorithms, a node validates new information with the existing information and provides a go or no-go signal. After the transaction is verified, a new block is added to the existing block of transaction, and it is copied to all the nodes on the network. As each node contain its own separate copy of information, there is no need for a centralized body of governance. This is why it is called a distributed ledger.

Chapter 34

Popular blockchains

The following are a few popular blockchains:

- **Bitcoin**: This is a decentralized digital currency or crypto-currency, which can be mathematically generated by executing complex number-crunching tasks. A money transfer is known as a Transaction and the process of generation is called Bitcon mining. A currency transfer is made with the help of a Bitcoin wallet and appropriate software. The entire process is monitored over the network with Blockchain technology.

- **Ethereum**: A programmable blockchain, Ethereum is a platform, that, unlike BitCoin, can be programmed by users as they wish. This gives freedom to developers/users to decide about the environment, whether a financial transaction, voting count, or any other industry where security is of key importance.

- **Keyless Signature Infrastructure (KSI)**: Guardtime, a cryptographic applications company, has developed a blockchain KSI that uses the concepts of digital signatures (a unique representation of a transaction) and digital fingerprints (a unique representation of a group of transactions at a specific time) for validation and verification.

Implication for testing

The validation of both functional and non-functional requirements should be done for blockchains like in any other application. Functional testing should focus on unit, integration and system testing, while non-functional testing should be focused on security and performance testing. The continuous integration and continuous delivery approach should be adopted where testing is done several times in a day, and a version control system should be used to keep tabs on updates. Service virtualization should be used to access virtual forms of the required testing stages.

Traditional testing processes are very slow and depend on manual testing scenarios. For blockchain testing, there is a dire need for testing teams to be very innovative and agile. Though organizations have started adopting agile, DevOps, and automation in their test approaches, effective implementation of these processes and insights about the level of risks associated with the application are always a challenge.

The blockchain ecosystem updates itself very frequently and, hence, requires a continuous testing approach that provides a continuous feedback of business risk in the application. Continuous testing puts the emphasis on extreme automation.

The following are the benefits of the continuous testing approach:

- Continuous feedback about a build or release
- Early testing leads to reduced time and effort in finding and fixing defects
- Time and effort saving allows teams to focus on other priority tasks, which can improve the quality of deliverables
- Frequent measurement helps teams to gather data related to metrics, which can be used for continuous improvement in the future

Conclusion

World quality report 2016-17 states that Blockchain and FinTech are accepted widely across industries. Aiming to achieve digital transformation and reduced time to market, quality assurance (QA) teams have to deliver results in a shorter timeframe and in a more complex technology environment. For achieving business objectives, the QA and testing teams needs to adopt agile, DevOps, and continuous delivery approaches with a special emphasis on the mindset of a new delivery paradigm. Adoption of these technologies and frameworks is expected to take a spike in 2017 as a lot of banks, financial institutions, and supply chain giants have started testing blockchain for their business processes.

35

Technologies for Digital Supply Chains and QA Considerations

The logistics, manufacturing, supply chain, and transportation industries are going through a time of rapid and unprecedented transformation. The future of these industries is paved with innovation and technology. It was not long ago that ideas such as 3D printing, the **Internet of Things (IoT)**, drone delivery, and augmented reality were things of science fiction. Today, merchants and service providers within these industries are cautiously adopting these technologies to provide faster, cheaper, more reliable, and sustainable business practices. Supply chains of organizations are leveraging these technologies to understand customer value chain and optimize their inbound and outbound logistics.

In this chapter, we will discuss:

- The non-linear journey of the customer buying process
- Business and technology trends in supply chain management
- New technologies in supply chain management
- Focus of QA in supply chain

Understanding the customer buying process

The consumers have evolved from transacting single channel to multichannel, cross-channel to omni-channel. The providers/marketers have enabled the business transition from single-channel to omni-channel. This evolution to omni-channel business has enabled cross-channel structure, flexible customer journeys, and single brand reinforcement:

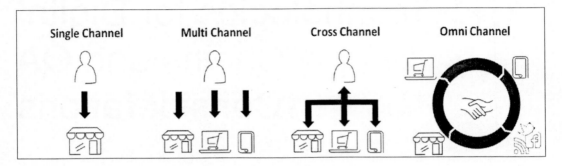

The customer in the digital age follows a non-linear journey, and for a single transaction, navigates across various store forms, physical out-of-store, digital out-of-store (at home, on-the go), digital in-store (own device, in-store devices), and physical in-store.

Take an example where a customer looks at a product in a physical catalog/printed ad, scans the QR code to get further details on the product and options, checks online social media feedback on-the-go, goes to the physical store and talks to a purchase consultant and checks the demo of the products, leverages web analytics data and recommends options/accessories suitable. Now, an in-store assistant uses a kiosk to check the availability of the recommended accessories not available in store, at other stores. The customer then uses his own tablet device, barcode scanner, and payment wallet to place the order and use the coupons. Finally, the item is picked up the same day from another store and delivered to the door. Finally, one of the accessories does not perform as intended; the malfunctioning item is collected from home. The customer puts a feedback about this on the customer service portal. Also, loyalty points are credited. One can see the customer has navigated across channels for one single transaction.

Industry trends in supply chain management

The **business trends** that impact supply chains include:

- Blurring of boundaries between industries — telecom, financial services, and retail
- Contiguous multichannel shopping experience
- Customer collaboration as a core competence in digital business
- Store as the multichannel execution hub of a digital business
- Digital workplaces of future with bring-your-own device, crowd-sourcing, and mobile workforce
- Executing multichannel fulfillment for competitive differentiation
- Focusing on customer-facing processes for business transformation
- Growing use of predictive customer analytics and intelligence

The **technology trends** that impact supply chains include:

- Combining digitalization with the Internet of Things
- Prioritizing the role of multichannel **Master Data Management (MDM)** and **Multichannel Content Management (MCM)** in digitalization and customer experience
- Deploying distributed order management to execute retailer multichannel fulfillment strategies
- Introducing smart machines (robots, drones) to improve productivity
- Focusing on in-store technology to execute the basics in a digital store
- Prioritizing data security to protect the brand
- Adopting desktop 3D printing services

New technologies in supply chain management

Supply chain management has undergone a significant change due to the varying demands of customers. New segments and new services are evolving day-by-day, which is making supply chain complicated. Some of the new technologies that are making supply chain more efficient and more optimized are outlined as follows:

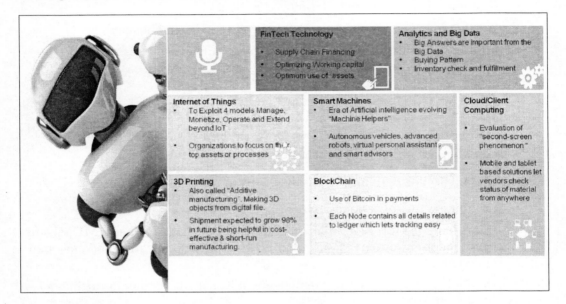

- **FinTech Businesses**: Supply chain financing is the biggest achievement of FinTech technologies in the supply chain sector. FinTech, also known as Financial Technologies, is a resonance of technology and financial services. Due to digitization, a new breed of companies has evolved, which promise customers to provide financial services online. This has helped companies to optimize their working capital and utilize their resources and assets in a better way.

- **Analytics and big data**: There is abundant data from every possible source. But big answers are required from big data, and here, analytics will come into the picture. Various analytical models are giving valuable suggestions to vendors and manufacturers about the buying patterns of customers. This helps in streamlining the supply chain and avoid supply chain conflicts.

- **Internet of Things (IoT)**: This has changed the way a material is shipped from a factory to a client. A set of sensors, with the help of software, track shipments and their conditions at each point of time. This helps in fighting problems such as time of delivery, climate change, demand and supply, and more.

- **Smart machines**: Making errors is a virtue of humans but not machines. Smart machines can do a particular job for us in a more efficient way than a human. This can make supply chain more agile and responsive. This will also help in optimizing the raw material costs.

- **Cloud computing**: The concept of second screen is coming into the picture these days. A new post of *Supply chain officers* has evolved in the recent time, who can track shipments from various devices or second screens and take immediate actions.

- **3D printing**: The use of different kinds of materials in 3D printing is changing the supply chain industry. Also called additive manufacturing (printing in layers), it can be a boon to fight situations such as demand-supply mismatch.

- **Blockchain**: FinTech disrupts the financial industry and Blockchain disrupts Fintech. Blockchain is a distributed database that holds records of digital data or events and keeps them tamper resistant. BlockChain is capable of tracking all types of transactions. Imagine a product that changes many hands till it reaches the end customer. If we can track all the events in the value chain, then costs and delays can be checked.

An illustration – new technologies in retail

We discussed business trends and emerging technologies in supply chain. Let's take an example of the retail industry and applicable technologies.

The following list provides a hype cycle:

- Innovation trigger
- Peak of inflated expectations
- Trough of disillusionment
- Slope of enlightenment
- Plateau of productivity

As can be seen from the following image, most of the technologies in retail would have their plateau either in 2-5 years or in 5-10 years:

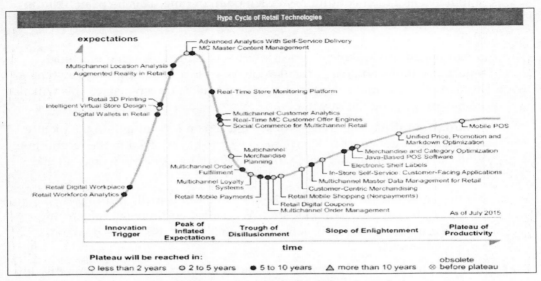

Source: Gartner Hype Cycle of Retail Technologies

Focus of QA in supply chain

The emergence of new technologies and platforms has significantly impacted customer centricity and a need for heightened customer experience. So, to be efficient as well as achieve customer satisfaction, enterprises are revamping their business processes, re-engineering, automating, and adapting them. The overall aim is to improve and optimize the business processes of an organization via automation, application development, integration, and maintenance to enable it.

Let's discuss the supply chain characteristics and the testing technique/type that provides an assurance:

- **Dynamic business processes**: Standard business processes are being replaced by adaptive processes. New processes focus on customer acquisition, retention, customer satisfaction, and turn-around time. Agile business processes are being designed so that process changes and course corrections can be handled quickly, in line with the market changes.

- **Shorter lead time for new product development and features**: Lead time for new products, features, and enhancements are reduced due to market changes, which, in turn, poses a challenge for testing to keep pace to ensure high quality, first time right fit for purpose.

- **Consistency, repeatability, and reusability of processes**: The need for reusable process components for minimal rework, ultimately facilitating faster turnarounds.

- **Customer experience / customer centric usability**: Personalized customer experience and optimizations in user interface lead to better customer retention and satisfaction. Testing around usability, accessibility, and performance will help enable this key aspect of digital transformation.

- **Compliance and security of business processes**: Securing business processes and making processes compliant to industry regulations are also the key paradigms of digital transformation. Refer to the following diagram:

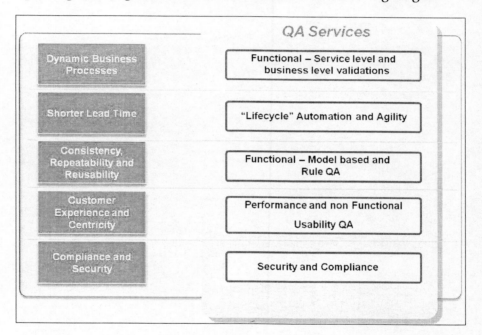

Conclusion

In summary, the use of modern technologies such as Fintech, IoT, Blockchain, cloud computing, 3D printing, smart machines, analytics, and big data are set to make supply chains more optimal and efficient. As devices and customer-facing mobile applications have changed the face of buying process, a smooth adoption of these technologies in various touch points in the supply chain holds the potential of enhancing efficiencies in various areas of the supply chain.

36

Potential Innovations in eHealth-Care – Implications for Testing and QA

Today, the emerging field of connected or digital healthcare is a reality. Connected healthcare is revolutionizing the industry by making diagnosis, treatment, and prevention widely accessible at a low cost. This will soon shift from fee-based to value-based care. With advancements in wireless technology, digital healthcare has set the stage for significant industry disruption. Digital health promises affordable, highly efficient, and easily accessible patient solutions.

In this chapter, we will discuss the following topics:

- Digital transformation trends in the healthcare sector
- Applications of digital eHealth-Care — remote patient monitoring, telehealth, and behavior modification
- Digital eHealth-Care ecosystem
- Typical challenges and need for a robust digital QA framework
- An illustrative customer journey validation of patients using wearables

Digital transformation trends in the healthcare sector

Before we begin to discuss the application of digital technologies in the healthcare sector, it is worth discussing excerpts from the **World Quality Report (WQR)** 2016, as applicable to the sector.

Considering the appointment (or the process of appointing) of chief digital officer as the key indicator of digital maturity, the healthcare sector was considered a laggard in 2016.

Healthcare organizations have been the largest users of private clouds, apart from the public sector.

In terms of the state of maturity in digital transformation, as per the findings of WQR 2016, the healthcare sector is not in the forefront of digital transformation; however, it has enormous scope. In this chapter, I will discuss the applications of digital healthcare, digital healthcare ecosystem, key challenges in digital eHealth-Care, the need for a robust QA, and the required customer journey validations.

Applications of digital eHealth-Care care

Key applications of digital eHealth-Care include the following:

- **Remote patient monitoring (RPM)**: We are witnessing the confluence of emerging technologies with healthcare and an increased awareness of our own bodies.

- Wearable pedometers and heart monitors have been around for years, letting people keep a track of how far they walk on a daily, weekly, or even monthly basis, further letting them track the amount of calories they are burning when they exercise. These devices also let people monitor their heart rates as most doctors advise raising your heart rate for at least 30 minutes every time you exercise. The newly released Apple watch has given wearers the ability to track an array of different types of health statistics. Such devices generate huge amounts of data that can potentially be used in conjunction with medical records, doctors, and hospitals to provide a better and more personalized level of service. And let us not forget new applications for the remote monitoring of chronic illnesses, and applications for remote diagnostics.

- **Telehealth**: If your phone is helping you to predict and prevent medical problems and providing a more intimate, personal level of service than your doctor ever could, your need for basic medical services and consultation will likely decrease. We will soon witness the next wave of personal technology tailored to our individual medical needs. Imagine that you have just undergone a major surgery; you have been released from the hospital and are recovering at home. You would need constant personal monitoring, visits from relatives and nurses, trips to and from the doctor, and a host of inconvenient tests. What if your smart watch could track your vitals and transmit the data in real time to your surgeon, your primary care physician, and the hospital where your surgery was performed? The transmitted data would be analyzed by custom software that could identify any extant or pending problems. If something serious were likely to happen, you would automatically be scheduled for an appointment and be sent a text letting you know when and where to come in for a checkup. Apart from being cost-effective for patients, it would be extremely convenient. The same idea can be applied to people with chronic or other serious diseases, such as diabetes, heart disease, or cancer.

- **Behavior modification**: Governments, insurers, employers, and most importantly, patients and their physicians recognize that digital technology is the key to meeting the challenges of healthcare provision in the 21st century. Cloud software, smartphone applications, online marketplaces, and data analytics are established technologies that the healthcare sector is embracing now. Digital technology is the key as healthcare seeks to become more efficient and patient-centric, paying for remote treatment and outcomes delivered with much care. More and more patients across the world are taking charge of their own healthcare. Hospitals, pharmacies, insurance companies, and medical professionals are finding themselves forced to adapt to this new wave of digital disruption or face losing patients and falling behind their competitors. Digital disruptive technology transformation and adoption for any healthcare organization needs a detailed assessment. Digital QA plays an important role as healthcare organizations are becoming more patient-centric.

Digital eHealth-Care care ecosystem

Let's first consider the healthcare ecosystem. Key entities, such as providers, pharmacies, payers, banks, insurance companies, and clearing houses, are depicted in the following figure:

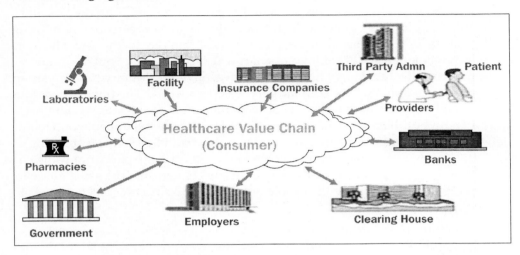

It is worth noting that four typical digital applications in eHealth-Care are in the areas of health information systems, digital pharmaceutical and life sciences, providers, and payers. A digital blueprint for eHealth-Care is visualized as follows:

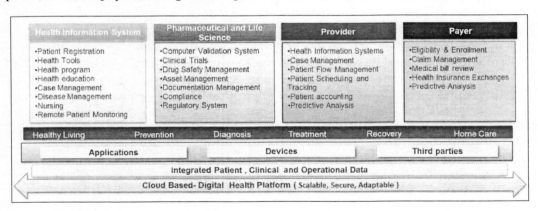

Typical challenges in digital eHealth-Care care

The key challenges faced in this ecosystem include the following:

- High frequency of changes and releases
- Validation of multiple channels for offering consistent user experience
- Ever-increasing regulatory compliance
- Data security and privacy concerns
- Concerns relating to the reliability and security of wearable devices

Need for robust digital QA

The earlier challenges need to be addressed through a robust digital eHealth-Care QA framework. Capgemini has developed a robust digital QA offering to cater to the eHealth-Care ecosystem. The offering includes the required QA and testing services to be performed for digital healthcare assurance. The following is a digital QA services overview:

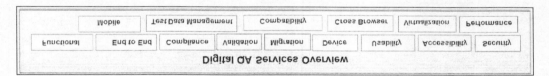

Digital eHealth-Care QA solution should offer the following things:

- A consistent and homogenous customer and user experience
- Agile testing for a faster time to market
- High performance through cloud-based solutions
- Secure application deployment

An illustrative customer journey validation of patient using wearables

The following illustration shows the customer journey validation steps for a patient with wearable devices:

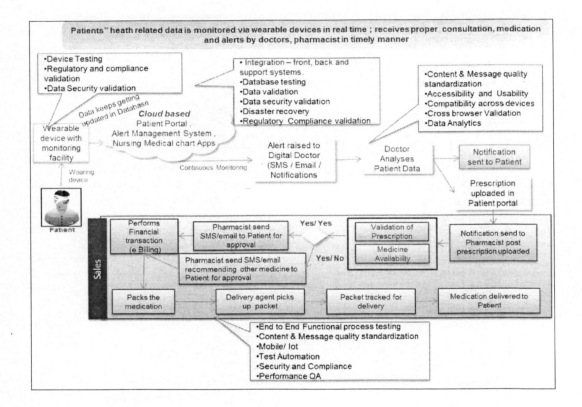

Conclusion

The digital eHealth-Care landscape is evolving and includes applications in health information system, pharma and life sciences, provider, and payer space. The eHealth-Care ecosystem has its own challenges and validation needs to address those challenges. A robust validation service incorporating functionality, usability, performance, compliance, migration, devices, compatibility, accessibility, security, and other aspects will the ensure successful deployment of digital eHealth-Care applications. A customer journey validation approach ensures that all the key touch points in the customer journey are validated.

For an in-depth look at the key trends in testing and QA, download the World Quality Report 2016 at `http://ow.ly/BEOh304rWx0`.

37

Trends in the Global Automotive Sector – Implications for Testing and QA

The automotive sector faces uneven demand, based on geographies and season. Globally, the demand has been impacted with shifts in consumer buying behaviour, expanded regulatory requirements, and increased information availability. China has been a key player in the automotive segment and the government in China is making significant infrastructure investments for the global automotive manufacturers to find it attractive to manufacture in China. Global strategies of OEMs, part suppliers, and dealers impact the automotive industry in China.

In this chapter, we will discuss the following topics:

- Business drivers for global automotive evolution, including consumer demand, regulatory requirements, and increased availability of information
- Key highlights from the growing Chinese automotive market
- Influence of global automotive trends on the Chinese market
- What do these trends mean for QA in the automotive segment

Business drivers for global automotive evolution

The demand for automobiles in the global market is uneven, with the strongest growth in North America, the weakest in Europe, and the most inconsistent in growing markets such as China and India. Against the current macroeconomic scenario, the following factors drive the future of the automobile industry:

- **Shifts in consumer demand**: Consumers are demanding more sophisticated and affordable infotainment systems and are expecting high-end features to be standard.

- **Expanded regulatory requirements**: Tighter **Corporate Average Fuel Economy (CAFE)** in the USA is driving for more safety, fuel efficiency, and emissions control.

- **Increased availability of data and information**: Information about vehicle usage and driver behavior is growing as sensors and telemetric systems become more accessible. This leads to innovations in car infotainment that are powered by car telematics. These leaps in technology, in turn, drive greater differentiation and attract customers from the competing brands. The increasing use of infotainment and telematics systems disrupts OEMs and traditional suppliers, changing the ways in which industry players design and develop new products and services.

Key highlights from the growing Chinese automotive market

The following data points highlight the importance of the Chinese automotive industry within the global landscape:

- 40% of BMW sales worldwide come from the Chinese markets, further emphasizing the importance of the growing Chinese luxury car industry

- Over 30% sales of Daimler worldwide come from the Chinese market

- Local Chinese brands are catching up with global brands, both in quality and brand share

- Global brands are eating into the local market, competing with Chinese brands in tier-2 and tier-3 cities in both the cost and value for money

- An upcoming wave of growth is expected from the electric vehicle sector due to increased government subsidies

- The local Chinese electric car market is experiencing a growth in double digits and foreign brands have yet to infiltrate this trend

- The Chinese government is making massive infrastructure investments so that automakers can penetrate tier 3, 4, and 5 markets by 2030

Influence of global automotive trends on the Chinese market

Global automotive trends significantly impact **Original Equipment Manufacturers (OEMs)**, as the following points outline:

- **OEM strategy**: Given the increase in electronic content, OEMs need to collaborate with suppliers and experts outside the traditional auto industry, including hardware and software companies. The importance of infotainment will drive OEMs to improve their skills to gather and analyze consumer data in order to serve their customers better and cultivate brand loyalty.

- **Supplier strategy**: Suppliers should partner with innovative non-traditional automotive electronics and infotainment suppliers in order to utilize both their speed to market and scale.

- **Dealer strategy**: As more buyers use online research, rating, price comparison, and offers, the dealers in turn need to invest in data management and customer care technologies. This will help facilitate the buying transaction, rendering it more efficient, less pressured, and more pleasing to buyers. Customer care technologies should extend to post-sales cycles, including servicing, vehicle health, proactive monitoring, and vehicle repurchasing to build loyalty and brand image.

The automotive manufacturing sector in China forms an important link within the overall automobile sector from OEM components to parts supply perspectives. Most of the global OEM players from Europe and the US have bases in China for manufacturing auto parts in order to fulfill the demand for domestic and international consumption.

For example, Chrysler has approximately 140 parts' suppliers in China from whom they purchase nearly $640 million worth of goods, representing 3% of its global purchases. The domestic consumption involves parts repurchase, replacement, and export, driven by global new car sales. The automotive suppliers in China need to increase the production of high-end infotainment products and scale up to the demands of both the global OEMs and domestic consumption. This will involve not only partnering with downstream electronics and infotainment suppliers, but also working with global OEM product rollouts, whose product release cycle is tightly integrated with the supplier parts' rollout cycle.

How are trends in automotive segments shaping software testing?

As per WQR 2016, the QA and Testing spend is predicted to increase to 40% of the overall IT budget by 2019. While this predicted upward trajectory must eventually halt, it is perhaps indicative of the industry's enthusiasm for emerging technologies and automation techniques. For example, 48% of survey respondents in this sector foresee using cognitive automation, and 40% foresee the use of predictive analysis (automated identification of the risk areas). Elements of these developments are already evident, with 47% of automotive sector respondents saying that they use predictive analytics to determine or optimize test coverage in a DevOps environment. This corresponds with findings from across all the sectors of an increasingly intelligence-led approach to test data and test environment management.

OEM suppliers need to increase their capabilities in digital testing on the application side, with a focus on IoT, analytics, artificial intelligence, **Platform as a Service (PaaS)** testing, and cloud platforms. On the technology side, key capabilities in automation, agile development, DevOps, and cloud testing become crucial differentiators for growth and sustainability. New capabilities in embedded testing, IoT testing, machine learning, and connected devices validations are required to holistically address the needs of infotainment and telematics systems.

Dealers also need to upgrade their systems in order to engage the customer effectively during pre and post-sales stages to digitize all the customer touch points. This will enhance the customer experience and drive the top line.

The following table illustrates how various vehicle finance providers are addressing the vehicle financing market in China with their digital strategy:

	SAIC GMAC	Volkswagen Financial services	TFS	GAC-Sofinco	Mercedes-Benz Financial
Online Touch Points	Website / WeChat / Weibo	Website / WeChat / Weibo	Website / App / WeChat / Weibo	Website / WeChat / Weibo	Website / App / WeChat
Credit line Evaluation	Y	N	N	Y	N
Loan Calculator	Y	Y	Y	Y	Y
Submit application intention	Y (2,915,063 people already participate)	Y	Y	Y	Y
Loan Solution Recommendation	N	N	Y	Y	Y
Online pre-approval	N	Y, should provide identity document number; 2,215 people already apply successfully	N	N	N
Application Process Convenience	Contact applicant in 24 hours after EOI (express of interest)	get results 3 days after submitting all personal document	No process time guarantee but display comprehensive needed documents and application process	30m minutes assessment feedback, supporting document templates download	unknown

System integrators need to acquire skills to test applications built on **social, mobile, analytics, and cloud (SMAC)** platforms. This testing capability must cover agile, DevOps, cognitive automation, predictive QA, cloud testing, IoT testing, and big data. Embedded system testing should cover the infotainment and telematics systems.

The global automotive market will see tighter integration and collaboration among OEM suppliers, system integrators, and niche technology companies to deliver on value.

Conclusion

Digital disruption and innovation in global automotives are driving the demand for the niche testing services of OEMs, OEM suppliers, system integrators, and ecosystem partners.

The emergence of connected cars is driving the convergence of application testing and embedded testing services to create seamless, end-to-end, digital testing.

Cognitive automation, DevOps, artificial intelligence, IoT testing, automated test environments, test data automation, and predictive QA will dominate the testing for the automotive segment. Traditional testing providers need to transform themselves to fit into the new age of digital by focusing on both the speed and the digital experience.

38

Digital Transformation in Consumer Products and Retail Sector – QA Considerations

With the increasingly competitive trading environment, **consumer products and retail (CPR)** companies are re-thinking their global operating model. It is clearly understood that deploying the right operating model leads to cost-effective operating platforms, improved market insight, and, thereby, improved competitiveness.

In this chapter, we will discuss the following:

- Current challenges in the CPR sector
- Key trends in physical and online stores
- Digital transformation in the CPR industry
- An illustrative customer journey of a digital shopper in an omni-channel environment
- An illustration of what *being digital* means for the CPR industry
- Factors considered by digital shoppers
- QA considerations and tests required in omni-channel CPR

Current challenges in the consumer products and retail sector

Today's consumer products and retail companies are operating in a very challenging economic environment with traditional retail shops taking a backseat and a growing population of tech-savvy consumers imbibing online shopping experience. A multitude of players in each of the categories of consumer products also throws up another challenge of a weak consumer confidence in these consumer product companies. Owing to this, each of these companies catering to a specific category of consumer products competes with one another to deliver a best-in-class experience for the consumers.

To add to the previous challenges, consumer products and retail companies have to deal with consolidation, discounting, and new channels, especially based on digital technologies. The changing customer needs and loyalty, the pressure of sustaining in these challenging environments, and the introduction of digital technologies has taken the rivalry to a different level altogether. Pure-play e-commerce retailers have grown significantly despite the increased rivalry and most traditional brick-and-mortar retailers struggle to incorporate these challenges in their business models.

Physical versus online stores – key trends

You can have a look at the brief overview of the trends in the market, which can broadly be classified and simply known as physical and online:

Brick-and-mortar – physical stores

Physical stores still enjoy a major market share as customers would like to feel the product before they buy (for example, jewelry, spectacles, clothes, sports equipment, and so on.). Most of the big retail stores have brought all the products under one roof, which makes them a one-stop shop for all the customer's needs. Currently, physical stores have staff to assist the customers in their purchase. Retail stores have a **Point of Sales (PoS)** system, which is integrated with all the other systems.

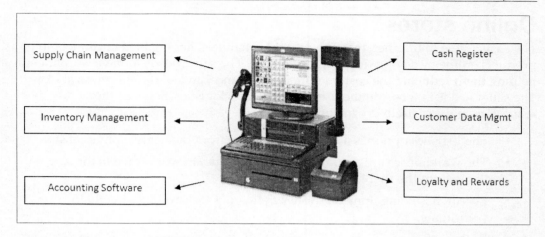

Supply Chain Management		Cash Register
Inventory Management		Customer Data Mgmt
Accounting Software		Loyalty and Rewards

The physical stores have been continuously upgrading themselves to the new technologies. The latest being

The trolleys are being fitted with a bar code scanner and all the items kept in the trolley are scanned for billing. This helps the customer to know the total cost of each time he/she places on the trolley.

All products are tagged with a magnetic strip in bar codes. When the trolley is moved across a scanner, it gives the total bill of all items instantly.

To help customers with the retail store map and deals, beacons are used. If the customer downloads the retail store app, he/she would be able to connect to the beacons and get details of the best deals available.

Amazon Go has come up with stores where billing clerks are not required. Customers with the Amazon app installed can scan their mobiles at the entry point and get into the store. Any product they pick up gets added to the cart and the product they keep back is removed from their cart, this is done using video cameras and sensors fitted across the stores. When they move out of the store, the products purchased gets billed to their account. This reduces the queues in the billing counter and no cashiers.

Cloth stores have come up with 3D capturing facilities for their customers and provide them multiple visual clothing options for their images. This helps the customer to decide their choice, rather than wearing the actual cloth. This is applicable to spectacles shops also.

Smart shelves help in alerting if the inventory is running low and in the instant updation of the product price on display.

Online stores

The easy access to Internet, through multiple channels, has enabled customers to buy products online by saving time and travel cost. The seller needs to have warehouses, helping them reducing the cost on rent, maintenance, and staff for a physical store. The seller needs to focus on the user interface and logistics. Some of the trends relating to logistics/delivery include the following:

- The logistics option is available to pick up from the nearest physical store
- The warehouses are automated, reducing human work force in moving the items from the shelves to the containers
- Research is being done on drones delivering the product directly to your home
- With driverless cars in an experimental stage, the future would be driverless vehicles coming to your home to deliver the products (drones might have a challenge in carrying heavier products)

Digital transformation in CPR industry

Digital transformation is being applied in the CPR industry in multiple areas, such as customer handling, content management, commerce management, and fulfillment, optimizing performance across channels to ensure seamless convergence of physical and digital channels. The following schematic highlights the various domains that have benefitted from digital technologies applied to the CPR industry:

Seamless convergence of physical and digital channels offers a relevant and personalized experience across all relevant touch points

Customer	Content	Commerce	Fulfilment	Performance
Managing a personal and relevant dialogue with individual customers	Managing high-quality and rich inspirational content across all channels and touchpoints	Managing maximised sales conversion leveraging optimal merchandising and pricing across all channels	Efficiently delivering the orders across all channels at the location and time your customers prefer	Optimising the performance of your business across all channels
Cross Channel Service Management	Web Content Management	E-commerce	Strategic Order Orchestration	Payment / Fraud / FX Management
Integrated Marketing & Campaign Management	Digital Asset Management	Digital Merchandising Management	Transport and Delivery management	Finance – Allocation and KPI's
Social Media Engagement	Product Information Management	Pricing & Promotion Management	Warehouse / 3rd Party Management	
Loyalty & Rewards			Returns Management	

With the advent of digital technologies into the sector, the consumer products and retail landscape is rapidly transforming as customers demand more information, access, and options than ever before. Being a shopper today is more exciting than ever. Shoppers are enabled with technology that allows them to approach the shopping process in a different way than they have in the past. Today's customers or digital shoppers demand for an always on and always open shopping experience.

- **Omni-channel, or all-channel retailing**: Generally defined as providing a customer with a consistent research, shopping, purchasing, and fulfillment experience regardless of channel or channels — is at the heart of this transformation. As a result, a clear omni-channel strategy, where essential components are seamlessly integrated, is increasingly becoming critical to the success of today's retailers.

- **Multichannel shopping**: With omni-channel retail being the talk of the time and technological advancement in the digital space percolating to every segment and age-group of the society, today's so called **digital shopper** is taking on shopping journeys that span across these channels, while expecting a seamless transition at the same time. This is usually termed as **multichannel shopping**. While different consumers follow different paths and utilize the channels for different reasons, they expect the retailer to remember their interactions and channel preferences and adjust the service accordingly.

Customer journey of a digital shopper in an omni-channel environment – an illustration

The customer shopping experience today is often a combination of a physical and an online store. A customer can look at an item in a store, buy it online, may post reviews online, can return physically to the store, and so on. The following schematic illustrates a customer's shopping journey:

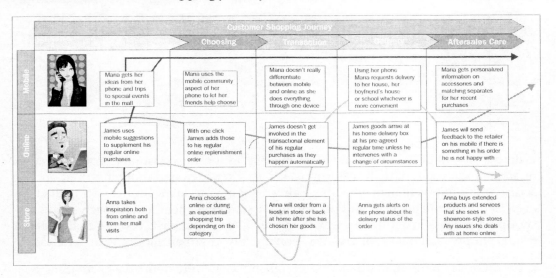

Being digital – what value levers can it offer to CPR industry

The CPR industry is more and more customer centric, and operates with an increased velocity/agility, while adapting to new technologies. Considering the key pillars of digital as mobile/channels, marketing, sales, business process management, and omni-commerce, the following schematic provides examples of digital transformation levers applied in each of these five areas to gain a competitive advantage:

		Customer Centricity	Increased Velocity and Agility	Adapt to new technologies
	Mobile & Channels	• Browsing through menu & placing order across any channel	• Seamless integration of inputs from various channels	• App based ordering
	Marketing Management	• Customized offers • Prioritized menu based on predictive analytics	• Digital communication • Social Analytics	• Offers through Geolocalization
	Sales Management	• App based delivery service	• Application of IoT and Robotics in delivery	• Virtual stores
	Commerce Management	• Multi channel payment options as per customer preferences	• Payment through online wallets, contactless cards, pre loaded cards etc.	• Payment through biometric authorization
	Business Process Management	• Localization and personalization	• Digital stores – virtual inventories	• Smart supply chain

Factors considered by digital shoppers

A research was conducted by Capgemini to figure out the criteria that are the most important for digital shoppers today and that are least important. The following table is a representation of the outcome of the research:

Options via Digital Channels	% of Consumers Saying "Extremely Important/ Extremely Appealing"
The product's price and availability are clearly marked	58%
Product delivery charges are clearly marked upfront	55%
Have products delivered to your chosen location	54%
Easily return products that you are not satisfied with using digital channels regardless of where purchased	50%
Choose from several different return options	49%

The criteria that matter less to the consumers are as follows:

Options via Digital Channels	% of Consumers Saying "Extremely Important/ Extremely Appealing"
Mobile app to support in-store shopping (for example, store map, special promotions)	21%
Shop with your friends online - looking and selecting together, although physically apart	20%
Be identified through digital devices when entering a physical store (through your mobile devices)	20%
Create public shopper profile visible to other shoppers in a retail digital channel	20%
Follow the retailer through social media	18%

Multi/omni-channel CPR – quality considerations

We discussed both physical stores and online stores. Digital transformation has more so increased the need for robust quality assurance. CPR industry applications require the number of verifications, which is as follows:

- Transaction verification (Verification of integration of point of sales terminal with cash registers, payment gateways, customer transaction history, and inventory):
- Verification of return and exchange of purchased items
- Physical inventory verification
- Verification of transactions in online store and payment gateway.

During a time, where there are a plethora of operating models and enabling technologies leading to cut-throat competition amongst consumer products and retail companies, even the slightest of a miss in either giving the best experience to its customers or an unforeseen technical flaw anywhere in the operations chain could cost the companies dearly. Therefore, digital QA takes the center stage in such times ensuring flawless operations and a delightful consumer experience. In order to meet these objectives, organizations must align their digital QA strategies to the four strategic levers that enable seamless consumer-centric operations.

Inventory visibility

It is vital for the retailers and consumer product companies to enable systems and processes to accurately track and manage their inventory throughout their supply chain network. This information should be of high quality and certainty. Therefore, companies are adopting EPC-enabled RFID to create pinpoint precision in their inventory accuracy, in a more real-time, dynamic way. This brings into picture the digital QA part, which needs to ensure that the RFID information is read accurately by readers and the information gathered is processed and utilized accurately. This data is then distributed across the globe to numerous connected devices, where IoT testing needs to be carried out to ensure end-to- end seamless operation.

Web-ready products

There is a demand for complete, accurate, and timely information about the products and services that the retailers and the consumer product companies need to sell. There is a need to improve the quality of information available and reduce the time to market. This information is required across all the channels and in parallel. For example, when a last item (product) is shipped, this information needs to be updated in the inventory management system which would then probably send a request/order to the manufacturer to ship the items to the warehouse, where the number of items to be shipped is decided by doing a predictive analysis of the customer buying behavior. Then, the information that the product is out of stock and would be available by a particular date needs to be updated in all the channels.

This overall scenario opens up many QA activities, which need to be carried out across each of these interfaces and also at the end points of these channels, such as mobile apps running on different platforms, PC-based apps, and the web interfaces of both these. In order to cater to these QA requirements, we need to have omni-channel QA as well. As security testing is also a vital aspect of QA when we have so many channels interfacing with each other.

Predictive customer analysis

The overall success of the omni-channel model is reliant on customer information being collected, stored, and utilized to anticipate the needs based on the past behavior of the customers. Companies then utilize the information for targeted promotions and offers and enhanced services of the products. This again requires a significant amount of QA going in to validate the analytics part itself, and also to validate that it meets the desired results at digital end-points of a shopping experience, such as devices, PCs, and browsers.

Fulfillment strategy

The goal is to provide the customer with the products they desire when, where, and how they want them, while enabling a seamless experience across channels. This necessitates end-to-end testing carried out to make the interactions between the interfaces appear seamless to the end customers. This also requires a lot of attention to be paid to the performance of each of these interfaces and all of them together. Therefore, QA activities to validate the performance at each level needs to be incorporated into the omni-channel QA strategy.

Digital transformation in CPR - tests required

There are a number of tests (validations) required that include functionality, adaptability, technology integration, accessibility, security, usability, ease of use, and performance. The following diagram provides the testing considerations and types of testing carried out for digital applications:

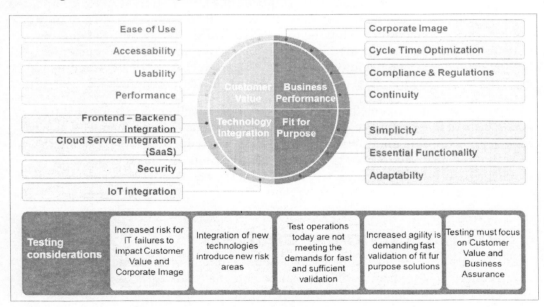

Conclusion

Customers continue to reshape the CPR industry using technologies that are readily available to them, and this is changing how and where products are sold. Consumers now want to experience an always-on, always-open shopping experience due to the accessibility offered by online shopping. Omni-channel fulfillment, therefore, requires an omni-channel QA strategy spanning across all the digital channels, ensuring a delightful end-to-end customer experience.

Conclusion

39

Digital Transformation Trends in Energy and Utilities – QA Considerations

The utility industry stands right on the forefront of adopting innovative technologies. Among utilities, for example, electric power, water, or transportation, the electric power utility industry is undergoing a momentous change. Digitalization and innovation drive the emergence of digital utilities business. **Chief Information Officers (CIOs)** in utilities sector must adapt their organizations to explore innovative provisioning business models.

Testing is an important component in a complex domain such as utilities. A regular trend of testing based on requirements does not help; the current market is looking for skilled resources who can understand the utility domain and can test many unwritten rules and end-to-end scenarios that cover the entire system involved in the utility application landscape. To overcome such challenges while testing these complex systems, understanding utility business scenarios and validating end user scenarios need intensive domain knowledge coupled with technology skills and experience.

In this chapter, we will discuss the following:

- Technology trends in the **Energy and Utilities Companies (EUC)** industry
- Key technology blocks of digital transformation in EUC
- Challenges of multichannel and the need for unified customer journey
- Key considerations in customer journey validation in EUC
- Illustration of QA considerations in **Smart Metering Infrastructure (SMI)**
- Digital Transformation QA trends in EUC

Technology trends in utilities industry

Socio-economic drivers and technology innovations, both are uniformly driving the utilities industry towards the digital world. The digital revolution is forcing change because it aggravates utilities' existing challenges and introduces new challenges. Digital disrupters are changing customer needs and behaviors. The following diagram illustrates the typical challenges the utility industry faces across various segments—residential and business (small, medium, and large):

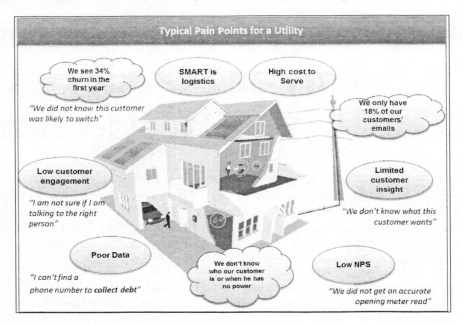

The energy and utilities industry is capital intensive and is likely to spend USD 40 trillion in the next two decades. The industry is looking to leverage the digital engagement channels to exceed customer expectations. The future technology adaptation areas in utilities will be around the use of social media, mobile solutions including mobile payments, big data analytics, digital marketing, **Internet of Things (IoT)**, and **Smart Meter Implementation (SMI)**. Smart metering has become the core of the utility business and meter data is the source of all measurements and analytics. These developments are the enablers of digital transformation for utilities.

IDC predicts that utilities will take on at least 40% of their earnings using new business models and services by 2017. The following are the list of pivotal areas in utilities future landscape.

- **Cloud**: By 2018, cloud services will make up half of the IT portfolio for over 60% of utilities

- **Integration**: In 2015, utilities will invest over a quarter of their IT budgets on integrating new technologies with legacy enterprise systems

- **Analytics**: By 2017, 45% of utilities' new investment in analytics will be used in operations and maintenance of plant and network infrastructure

- **Mobility**: 60% of utilities will focus on transitioning enterprise mobility to capitalize on the consumer mobility wave

- **Smart systems**: By 2018, cognitive systems will penetrate utilities' customer operations to improve service and reduce costs

Key technology blocks of digital transformation in the EUC sector

Major technology trends drive the digital transformation with composite solutions addressing business opportunities. In the past few years, digital transformation was just a buzz word, but today it is the fastest evolving opportunity that everyone is looking at, and utilities too. Mobility, intelligent devices, big data, and business process management systems constitute the digital ecosystem for utilities to deliver customer experience, operational efficiencies, and changing business models.

The following figure illustrates the key technology blocks for digital transformation in the EUC sector:

Service Provider(s)	Cloud Services	Home & Mobile Apps	Home Gateway & Appliances
• Marketing & Analytics • Customer Management • Partner Management • Service Provision	• Device Activation • App Downloads • Automation (scenes) • Messaging and Alerts • Customer & Partner Admin • Data Capture & Reporting	• Billboard • Energy Management • Comfort • Security • Healthcare • Widgets	• Gateway • Smart Meter • Thermostat • HVAC • Devices & Appliances
Integration with cloud, business change, customer recruitment and support	Managed business service	App customisation and development	Device driver development, vendor management

Challenge of multichannel and the need for a unified customer journey

Digital adoption comes hand-in-hand with the use of multiple channels. Multiple channels cause challenges that need to be addressed through adequate validation. Some of the characteristics pertaining to multichannel systems includes the following:

- Customer experience consistency
- Responsive design
- Handling of dynamic content
- Performance of the systems
- Bi-modal interfaces (digital/non-digital)
- Interface with point-of-sale devices
- Frequent releases
- Cyber security
- End-to-end validations

In summary, the key challenge lies in finding skilled members to perform the multichannel interface testing. The validations involve both the correctness of aggregated data results and the validation of the performance of the systems.

In the digital world, utilities are striving to serve the customers across channels and provide unified customer experience. The following figure provides a narrative of all the steps in the customer journey, for example, join, leave, move, pay, save, renew, raise service ticket about outage, and so on, using multiple channels:

Testing considerations in an EUC customer journey – an illustration

The next schematic depicts the various events in customer life cycle that a customer engages with the utility, leveraging multiple channels, such as e-mail, mobile, POS, mail, online, social networks, IVR, and so on. Various events depicted here include customer acquisition, consent, product/tariff change/update, connection/disconnection requests, meter exchange, payment option change/update, meter mode change, customer home move journey/change of tenancy (move in/move out). Given the challenge of multi-channel interfaces discussed in section (3) earlier, the required validations have been suggested, such as:

- UI/UX validation
- Multi-device compatibility
- Data security
- Cross-browser

- Localisation
- Performance
- IVR
- Accessibility
- Usability

Refer to the following diagram:

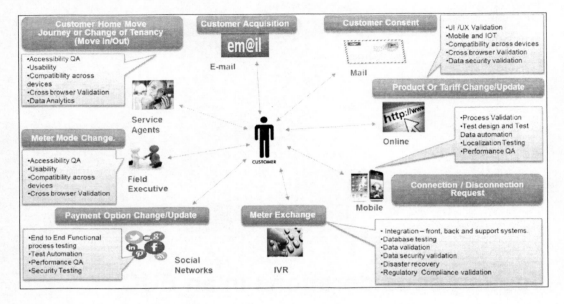

Testing considerations in smart metering infrastructure – an illustration

SMI implementations are gigantic projects with multiple programs running in parallel to achieve the overall objective. An SMI implementation results in significant new and improved business processes. SMI implementation consists of multiple components, which include smart meters, meter data management system, communication infrastructure, and their integration with existing utility systems, such as the customer profile, billing/CIS systems, Outage Management System, Geographical Information Systems, analytics, and other applications.

SMI testing involves an extent of activities to ensure that each individual components of the system meets the business requirements and to make sure that the integration of end-to-end systems are working as expected. Hence, there is scope for multiple testing activities across different technical areas in SMI implementation. Testing of the software components is a critical success factor in the overall smart meter deployment program.

Key testing areas in SMI implementation are:

- Billing system post AMI implementation
- Testing of Meter Data Management System
- Data migration and data warehouse testing
- Outage management
- Geographical Information Systems

Validating web portal upgrades in multiple devices such as mobiles and tabs (my account, customer usage, account and billing, rate plans, payments and credits, reports and analytics, demand response and demand-side management).

The following schematic provides a framework for testing smart metering implementation across functional areas such as meter deployment, operational support, distributed generation/demand side management, customer service/billing and various validations require:

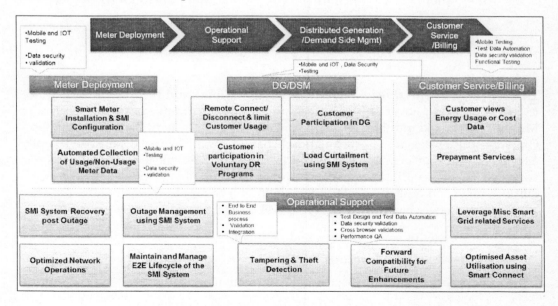

Digital transformation QA trends in EUC

As per WQR 2016, a key technology change associated with digital strategies is cloud adoption. Cloud-based provisioning and services have been slow to catch on within the utilities industry for the past few years, but they catching up the momentum in recent years. Along with digital, the utilities industries will focus on cyber security too.

On the operations side, forecasting comes to the forefront even more than anything from the past 15 years. The executives in utilities are trying to manage their grids, tying to figure out how to handle data, to figure out how to position the need for the future. Today, most of the industries are relying significantly on data-driven decisions. The utility industry is in need of analyzing demand forecast programs. They are looking for feasible choices, looking for optimum solution for the need, which is going to give them the best information and solution. Many of the large utilities are still running on legacy programs aged 30+ years, doing the same forecasting that they had used way back in the 1980s.

QA and testing play a vital role to evidence the digital transformation in utilities industry. As per WQR 2016, study findings reveal that testing new digital implementations is causing specific test challenges.

The most challenging aspects of testing digital implementation are:

- Integration services (including local, private, and public cloud)
- Multichannel interface (mobile, social, and traditional)
- Data and service orchestration
- End-to-end workflows

To test **SMACT** items (**Social, Mobile, Analytics, Cloud, and IoT**), organizations need to move towards innovative approaches, methodologies, frameworks, and accelerators. Multiplatforms and multidevice testing are the key aspects in digital transformation. Crowd testing/weekend testing and omni-channel/multichannel testing can be opted as one of the testing techniques to test social, cloud, and mobile requirements. To validate the various utilities applications across a group of interconnected devices, omni-channel and multichannel testing would be a better technique to move on. There are a few challenges cited in WQR 2016 in SMACT testing:

- Lack of right testing process and methods
- Demand for mobile testing experts
- Necessity of an in-house testing environment
- Hunt for best-fit tools for multichannel application testing

QA organizations need to concentrate more on providing concrete solutions for the aforementioned challenges to keep their momentum in the digital world.

Conclusion

Due to competitive market pressures, many of the utilities companies have experienced a significant cut down in their operational costs and, specifically, in their IT budgets. The utilities sector is still at the heart of a major structural transformation. The utilities industry finds the IT requirements challenging for digital transformation. In order to fulfill the critical role during digital transformation, QA organizations should have a comprehensive digital assurance platform.

References

- Capgemini Sogeti HP World Quality Report - `http://www.worldqualityreport.com/`
- IDC FutureScape: Worldwide Utilities 2015 Predictions

40
Smart Energy and Smart Grids – in Need of Effective Testing

The advent of digital technologies has been phenomenal for electric utilities. Electric utilities have seen transformation from the legacy systems to **Smart Grids and Smart Metering Infrastructure (SMI)**. While digital technologies have been a boon for electric utilities, the drivers for change have been cost pressures combined with a regulatory push.

In this chapter, we will discuss the following:

- Drivers for transformation of electric utilities
- Trends in Energy and Utilities (E&U) industry
- Key challenges in E&U
- Smart meters and Smart Grids
- Testing considerations for Smart Metering Infrastructure (SMI)

Background

Smart meters are playing a critical role in shaping the electric grids of tomorrow and enabling the integration of new, grid-related technologies. As the power grid evolves into a broad platform for integrating new energy services and technologies, the ability to connect legacy assets to systems and integrate new ones is critical. Smart meters are supporting this evolution. In addition, the data collected by smart meters (or **Smart Metering Infrastructure (SMI)**) opens the door for greater integration of new resources and new energy services for customers. The utilities transformation will eventually take **Business As Usual (BAU)** internal processes into more digitized event-driven processes, which will be governed by connected Grid sensors, digitally connected **In Home Devices (IHD)**, and smart meters.

The following diagram illustrates how regulatory push and cost pressures could transform the electric utilities of today into the digital utilities of tomorrow:

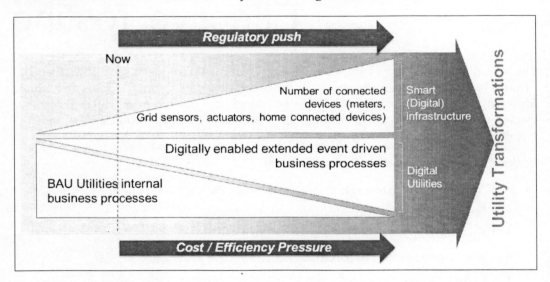

Trends in Energy and Utilities (E&U)

The IT landscape of energy and utilities is becoming more and more digital. However, there is not yet a clear consensus on digital transformation objectives, such as the desire to embed customer experience at the heart of the business strategy and the need to deliver operational improvements.

Key drivers to smart energy services trends include the following:

- Continued industry restructuring (demand side participation)

- Fast-paced smart initiatives: smart grid technology and smart meter installations

- Real-time grid analytics, digitization helping utilities interact with customers effectively and efficiently

- Energy savings through online campaigns and electronic channels

- Online customer interaction and social network collaboration

- Analyzing the consumer's behavioral patterns and quickly addressing the issues through the use of social networking and online interaction

- Challenge of meeting the renewable energy management targets

- Hitting the 2030 target of renewable energy-based electricity 99.9% of the time at rates comparable to those of today

The leaders recognize the need for cloud strategies and have started defining a timeline for migrating non-SCADA, **Supervisory Control and Data Acquisition systems (SCADA)** or software application program for process control, the gathering of data in real time from remote locations in order to control equipment, and conditions utility industry systems to the cloud, ensuring a 30-40% reduction in the cost of infrastructure setup.

Installed at a remarkable pace, about 300 million smart meters programs have been deployed so far, with the number to be jumping to a potential 1 billion in 2025. Customers need smart meters that work in real time using a two-way communication. Furthermore, Smart Home technology capabilities are being built into this area, focusing on both QA and testing.

Increased energy efficiency has reduced the need for energy consumption, while the distributed generation of renewables has increased the overall supply. Smart grids are responsible for balancing load and demand as shown in the following diagram:

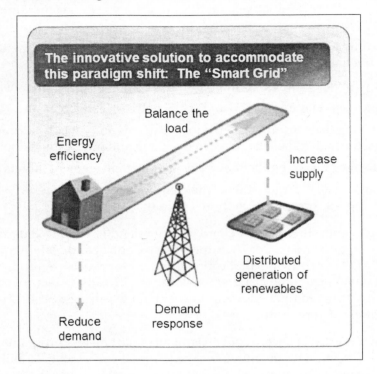

E&U Trends – References from WQR 2016

As per WQR 2016, 27% of the survey participants from the E&U segment indicate having added a dedicated Chief Digital Officer. 19% suggest that their digital transformation is in the hands of their IT leadership (CIO). 8% indicate that digital transformation resides within the business leadership.

43% of survey participants in the E&U segment are already testing both the user interface and the ease of use of mobile applications, and 17% of the QA and testing budget is spent on mobile solutions. 48% of respondents say that they do not have the right testing process or method for mobile and multichannel testing.

Cyber security for energy grids is an area in need of attention. 52% of survey participants indicate concern about the security of sensitive data on the device or over the air; this is more than in any other aspect of mobile testing, especially for field-based workforce.

Typical challenges in the E&U segment

Typical challenges in the **Energy and Utilities** (E&U) segment include the following:

- **An aging work force**: The high labor force participation rates are in the 55 to 64 age group. Furthermore, we have an aging infrastructure (investor-owned utilities will need to make infrastructure investments in the competitive market).

- **Environmental concerns**: The climate scientists expect *dangerous climate change* sometime between 2025 and 2030, which will be followed by strict regulations.

- **Energy technology consumerization**: The utility customers are adopting new energy-focused technologies, such as rooftop solar, **plug-in hybrid electric vehicles (PHEVs)**, and intelligent thermostats.

- **Cyber Security Concerns**: Smart meter data will raise many privacy and data protection issues that will also need to be addressed by utilities.

- **Failures in smart grid implementation**: Failure pertain to integration of **Outage Management System (OMS)**, **Distributed Management System (DMS)**, SCADA systems.

- Uncertain regulatory environment.

- Demand response and pricing: Consumers are keen to reduce their electric bills and target energy saving mechanisms.

Smart Meters and Smart Grids

With 300 million smart meters deployed, utilities are now focused on integrating and optimizing information gathered by smart meters and transmitted by **Advanced Metering Infrastructure (AMI)** communications systems, as well as from other investments in the digital grid, to provide benefits and new capabilities to customers and system operators. AMI systems integration with **Outage Management Systems (OMS)** and **Distribution Management Systems (DMS)** is providing enhanced outage management and restoration with improved distribution system monitoring.

Smart meters position the grid as a platform for the integration of energy resources such as distributed generation, community solar, electric vehicles, storage, and micro-grids. Smart metering gives customers real-time consumption information via display devices that translate the meter reading into a language the customer can easily understand. These devices help customers change their consumption habits without waiting for the end of the month or the end of the quarter to view the results from conservation initiatives.

A smart metering landscape includes the transportation of data from meters using various communication channels (for example, GPRS and RF Mesh). There is a layer of MDM that stores and carries out various functions such as **Validation** and **Estimation**. The meter data is used for various services such as billing, asset, and work management. The communication of the meter data to the back-end system occurs through an integration layer. Therefore, a typical smart metering landscape includes a range of solutions and products that include systems for data collection, **Meter Data Management** (**MDM**) systems, multiple integration layers, and the back-end ERP systems, the latter involving a mix of legacy systems.

The term Smart Grid refers to a modernization of the electricity delivery system. It monitors, protects, and automatically optimizes the operation of its interconnected elements. It starts from the central and distributed generator and moves through the high-voltage transmission network and distribution system, to industrial users; from building automation systems to energy storage installations, end-use consumers and their thermostats, electric vehicles, appliances and other household devices. Smart Grid technology affects many applications and system integration. From a testing perspective, this results in a work that is executed in multiple streams, components, and phases. Smart grids help to provide metrics data on distribution, resource allocation, and energy consumption.

Testing process for Smart Metering Infrastructure (SMI)

The complex nature of the E&U infrastructure calls for special attention and testing at each point, and such testing is susceptible to failure. Special attention also must be given to issues regarding security, data integration, technology compatibility, convergence, and performance.

The scope of a smart metering testing program includes integration testing, performance and availability testing, factory and site acceptance testing for the meter and grid data collection, and management systems as well as operational business process testing. Take a look at the following block diagram:

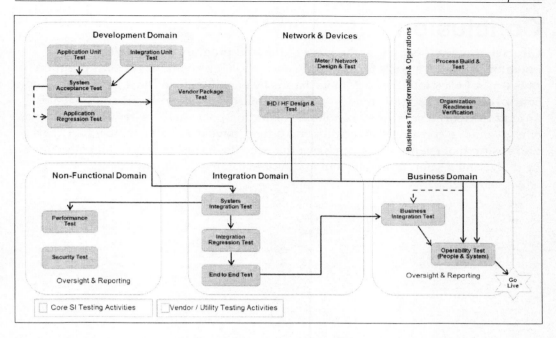

In the overall process of testing, individual application teams perform the complete development / Unit Testing and **System Acceptance Testing (SAT)** for SMI in-scope systems. **System Integration Testing (SIT)** scope is conducted by the System Integration test team. The business team of the program contributes in **Business Integration Testing (BIT)** (also known as User Acceptance Testing) with management, technical, and SME support provided by the Integration and test team. It includes test planning, scripting, and execution for each release/sub-release. Testing around meter networking, organization readiness, and IHD falls under the specific vendor and service providers.

While the System Integration test team has the accountability for the acceptance of the SMI deliverables from the quality assurance perspective, there are some areas that will not be tested by the System Integration test team. For all such areas, the System Integration test team reviews the testing reports and conclusions from the individual work streams and/or vendors that performed the testing. The SI testing checks the maturity from all areas of testing as highlighted in the above diagram. Sub-system maturity, as reported by all test teams involved, will feed in to the overall maturity radar of the System Integration test team.

Conclusion

Clean energy leadership is at the heart of the SMI program and enables utility operators to achieve goals for self-sufficiency and conservation. The SMI program puts control back into the customers' hands by enabling them to view, manage, and control energy use to save money. To make smart energy and smart cities a reality around the world, various stakeholders, including policymakers, regulators, utilities, cities, vendors, consumer advocates, and others, have to collaborate together. This will ensure that eventually, we achieve the benefits of smart energy and smart cities by delivering a safer, more-efficient and more-sustainable way of living.

41
Testing Airline Digital Applications – Case for Responsive Design

Tech-savvy consumers have increased mobility and want convenience of using all their gadgets at the convenience of home, when in transit, or travel. Airlines are fast adopting to digital technologies to provide a seamless customer experience.

In this chapter, we will discuss the state of the airline business, the role of digitization, and QA and testing, with the focus specifically on testing for implementation of business rules, system integration, non-functional testing, and testing for responsive web design.

Background – the state of the airline business

The global airline industry continues to grow rapidly, but consistent profitability remains elusive. Airline industry revenues have doubled in the last 10 years, reaching a value of USD 746 billion in 2014, according to the **International Air Transport Association (IATA)**. In the commercial aviation sector, just about every player in the value chain — airports, airplane manufacturers, jet engine makers, travel agents, and service companies — have experienced profits. However, the airline industry struggles to break even, with some airlines going out of business. Individual commercial airline responses to global trends will determine carrier performance in the coming years.

Airport operators also face additional challenges. Not only do they make sure that planes run on time, they also ensure the smooth, daily movement of passengers in large numbers across multiple terminals. Travelers today are very tech-savvy; they want to have all their gadgets function as if at home in order to be able to conduct digital activities during travel as they would at home or at work. Consumer disaffection is challenging for carriers to address. However, there is good news! If upgrading the actual aircraft or *hard product* presents an expensive path toward differentiation and a long payback period, enhancing the service or *soft product* through seamless customer experience is the way for airline carriers to raise their profitability. This calls for serious digital transformation efforts, some of which are already underway at many airlines.

Role of digitization

The digital revolution has peaked and is now altering traditional industries such as utilities, industrial goods, and airlines, among others. Executives in these industries recognize that sensors, machines, and IT systems can be connected to analyze data, enabling faster, more flexible, and more efficient processes. However, many of these executives struggle to understand how they can create strategic advantages by adopting digital practices.

At many airports, digital technologies and services are improving the passenger experience beyond mobile boarding passes and text message alerts. The business processes impacted by digital transformation fall within the purview of Airline Digital BPM.

With much of this transformation happening across processes, the quality of the product is important. Testers are constantly revamping traditional testing strategies, just as carriers devise ways of facilitating the adoption of these changes. In this chapter, we will explore both quality assurance and testing of airline digital applications. Take a look at the following diagram:

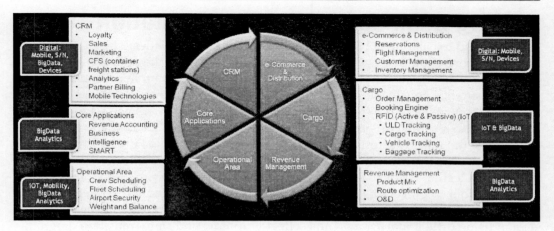

QA and testing in the airline industry

Changes in customer behavior and increased global competition are the two key challenges currently facing the airline industry. Adapting to social media channels, cloud, and mobile technologies is a way for airlines to cope with these challenges. More and more travelers book airline tickets online, and this requires travel agencies and airlines to focus on the customer experience their websites provide. Quality assurance and testing play a critical role in ensuring that business conducted online results in a smooth customer experience that is secure and reliable. It is important for airline carriers to have an appropriate digital assurance strategy by identifying the right tools, methodologies, and measures to implement a seamless customer experience. From our experience, there are three important factors to consider when seeking high quality airline software testing: business rules implementation, system integration, and non-functional testing.

Testing business rules implementation

Airlines need to customize business, packaging, and pricing rules. These customizations should be accurately implemented as part of the online booking process. Parameters such as passenger amount limitation, infant tax calculation, selling insurance policy, and loyalty service each have their own respective business rules and contribute to the complexity of test case design. Testers need domain knowledge to test the implementation of business rules. The ticketing process is not always a serial flow. A number of business rules within the booking process need to be considered when creating test strategy. From a quality perspective, airline application testing needs to ensure both adherence to industry regulations and ease of use in order to prevent user mistakes. The airline application test strategy needs to account for user preferences — including browser and behavior — and robust test case design using orthogonal arrays, cause effect graphing, and state transition diagram techniques depending on user scenarios and application functionality.

Systems integration testing

Travel booking services are usually based on one of the following platforms: **Global Distribution System (GDS)**, otherwise known as **Computer Reservation System (CRS)** and the **Internet Booking Engine (IBE)** combined with a payment system. Each of these components has evolved in complexity and has more and more functionality, making it critical to integration. The requirements need to be specified clearly as well as early. GDS, CRS, and payment systems have very strict performance tolerances. Slow responses when retrieving information may result in the user interface not rendering correctly or a failed ticket transaction and as such, seamless integration with low overhead is essential.

Non-functional testing

The way people access web applications is changing. It is no longer restricted to browsers on a laptop or desktop; tablets or mobile phones with varying screen sizes represent additional formats used for consuming information and carrying out transactions. In order to keep a user on your website or application, aesthetics and ease of usability are key components about which businesses should be concerned.

Testing responsive web designs

Responsive web designs are being used for building attractive web applications. They make your webpage look good on all devices: desktops, tablets, and phones. Responsive web design is about using CSS and HTML to resize, hide, shrink, enlarge, or move content to make it load effectively on any screen.

Responsive design results in the following benefits:

- It provides an optimal viewing and interaction experience with easy reading and navigation with a minimum of resizing, panning, and scrolling across a wide range of devices

- It provides consistent UX and coverage across all digital platforms

- It supports end-user workflow across multiple screens

- It can handle any new OS or platform release

- It consolidates resources and aligns business goals across platforms

Most software applications developed today are responsive. Manually testing responsive applications across multiple platforms is time consuming. That's why there is a need for a responsive automation framework that can complete automated responsive checks on the application, draft mock-ups, and report failures.

Given the multiple channels needed to access responsive design applications, automation is required in order to reduce the time to test. Traditional automation tools fail to test such dynamic web pages. One system, the selenium web driver, is a powerful tool to combat these shortcomings, thanks to its UI element identification flexibility. Furthermore, many commercial tools inherited older identification methods such as XPath and CSS. It is, however, the creation of select functions that may help support logical interactions with web applications. The **Galen** framework, an open source platform, offers a simple solution by testing the location of objects relative to one another on a webpage.

Using both special syntax and comprehensive rules, one can accurately describe any layout. With these tools, Capgemini has developed an innovative framework that integrates both **Selenium** and **Appium** while providing screenshot-driven reports for each validation in HTML format as shown in the following diagram:

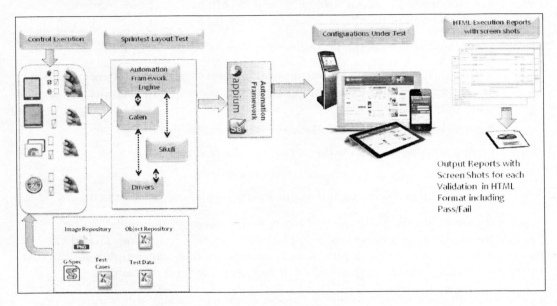

Automation Framework for Responsive Web Design

Conclusion

The airline industry has long struggled with profit margins. However, the current market attitude, coupled with evolving technology and customer preferences, may offer a real opportunity for growth and development. Yet this growth can only occur if the industry adopts the measures described in the preceding sections. Independent testing in the travel and hospitality sector calls for deep expertise in testing applications across critical functions. These include passenger services, fighter operations, e-commerce, maintenance, airport operations, and revenue management. These testing solutions must be equipped with checklists, testlets, frameworks, processes, methodologies, and best practices in order to ensure both effective and efficient validations.

Quality assurance needs to cover functionality, life cycle automation, usability, security, compliance checks, and non-functional aspects such as performance and reliability, all while reducing time to market. This can help forge better relationships with customers, cut costs, and improve overall financial performance. Airline carriers have choice to do this through in-house IT or by leveraging suitable technology partners.

42

Orthogonal Array Testing (OAT) – an Application in Healthcare Industry

The **Healthcare and Lifesciences (H&LS)** industry faces stringent statutory compliance requirements, making robust testing of applications a very crucial task. How much testing is adequate is always a question.

In this chapter, we will discuss challenges facing the H&LS industry, the need for robust testing, and use of the **Orthogonal Array Testing (OAT)** technique to optimize testing, and use of the OAT tool.

Background

The **Healthcare and Life Sciences (H&LS)** industry is driven by the stringent regulatory compliance needs, emerging protocols, and adherence to global standards. This has made software testing a challenging and an expensive proposition. Besides, the regulatory guidelines mandate upgradation of software system in a time-bound manner without compromising on patient safety. This has put tremendous pressure on product vendors and IT service providers to offer a quick turn-around time along with quality solution to remain competitive in business.

Challenges in H&LS applications testing

H&LS applications testing needs robust coverage and therefore has a need for optimization due to massive data and test conditions.

Large number of combinations of various parameters make it easy to miss a few critical data combinations.

Interaction and integration points as a major source of defects—most defects arise from simple pair-wise interactions.

Random selection of values create pair-wise combinations, which is bound to create inefficient test sets with random, senseless distribution of values.

Huge amount of effort with long testing cycles needed for exhaustive testing.

The H&LS industry faces fast changing regulatory compliance requirements such as the following:

- Stringent regulatory compliance needs, emerging protocols, and global standards make software testing challenging and expensive for the H&LS industry
- Time-bound upgrades for the software systems need to be carried out in a time-bound manner without compromising on patient safety
- New software solution needs to be quickly validated for correctness before being released to the market
- Changes in regulatory compliance lead to change in processes, which in turn leads to more testing and validation

The H&LS service providers are challenged by the fast changing regulatory requirements on one hand and shortened test cycle times for drug trials on other hand. The providers are facing a daunting task to revamp their entire testing strategy for quicker time to market.

How can Orthogonal Array Testing Strategy (OATS) help?

The data intensive test conditions can be optimized for better coverage and increased quality using **Orthogonal Array Testing Strategy (OATS)**:

- OATS is described as follows:
  - ○ It is a systematic, statistical way to test pair-wise interactions, especially in data-intensive test conditions
  - ○ It guarantees testing the pair-wise combinations of all the selected variables
  - ○ It creates an efficient and concise test set with fewer test cases than testing all combinations of all variables
  - ○ It creates a test set that has an even distribution of all pair-wise combinations
  - ○ It exercises some of the complex combinations of all the variables

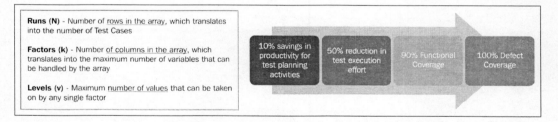

Runs (N) - Number of rows in the array, which translates into the number of Test Cases

Factors (k) - Number of columns in the array, which translates into the maximum number of variables that can be handled by the array

Levels (v) - Maximum number of values that can be taken on by any single factor

10% savings in productivity for test planning activities

50% reduction in test execution effort

90% Functional Coverage

100% Defect Coverage

- The benefits of OATS are as follows:
  - ○ Technology and domain agnostic test case optimization helps in reducing testing efforts
  - ○ It deploys pair-wise independent combinatorial testing algorithm to identify the optimized set of test cases
  - ○ It provides flexibility to change the depth of the combinations and also enables to define business rules

A typical OAT tool offers a technology and domain independent case optimization framework, which helps in reducing testing efforts. Our experience suggests ability to offer 90% test coverage with only 40% test cases. Algorithms such as **Microsoft PICT** can be used to identify the reduced test cases and offer flexibility to change the depth of the combinations and define business rules. The following diagram provides overview of an OAT tool:

- A typical OAT tool performs the following:
  - Guarantees testing the pair-wise combinations of all the selected variables
  - Creates an efficient and concise test set with fewer test cases than testing all combinations of all variables
  - Generates a test set that has an even distribution of all pair-wise combinations
  - Exercises some of the complex combinations of all the variables
  - Generates less error prone test sets than the ones created manually
  - Helps identify optimal test data sets

OAT can reduce a test set of 24000 (for 7 factors with 5 values) to 33 (for 2 levels) or 730 (for 4 levels) or 2746 (for 5 levels) as shown in the following screenshot:

Let us consider a test condition with 3 Factor and 2 Levels (sets of data) for each Factor.

Factors	Patient Age Group	Dosage	Outcome
Levels	A (21-30)	1 (5 mg)	S (Success)
	B (31-40)	2 (10 mg)	F (Failure)

In conventional testing technique, the number of test cases will be 8

	Patient Age Group	Dosage	Outcome
Test 1	A	1	S
Test 2	A	1	F
Test 3	A	2	S
Test 4	A	2	F
Test 5	B	1	S
Test 6	B	1	F
Test 7	B	2	S
Test 8	B	2	F

By applying OATS, the number of test cases will be reduced to 4

	Patient Age Group	Dosage	Outcome
Test 1	A	1	S
Test 2	A	2	F
Test 3	B	1	F
Test 4	B	2	S

OATS helps us to reduce the number of test cases by 50%, but at the same time it tests all the pairwise combinations

Conclusion

With constant advances in the H&LS industry and discoveries of new drugs, changes in sourcing, and increased regulations, the H&LS industries need innovative software testing methodologies to keep them agile and help them address specific needs. The testing strategies such as OAT are important tools for these organizations to keep up with the trends and stay competitive.

43

Future of Consulting in the Era of Digital Disruption

In the 1990s, when I passed my MS in Management from one of the top B-Schools in the USA, I considered management consulting as the top choice for my career. Being a woman, I was cautioned by several friends and well-wishers that the consulting career meant living out of a suitcase and a globe-trotting job to be a true partner to the clients.

The world of consulting in those years seemed very rich, I enjoyed juggling the domestic assignments in management and IT consulting across industries covering business process improvement, strategic and operations consulting including supply chain optimization, cost reduction, to name a few. Some of the hot IT consulting areas included **Enterprise Resource Planning (ERPs)**, IT health assessment, IT Packaged product selection, helping customers with authoring their requests for proposal for IT services, and so on. Then came the e-commerce boom in the 2000s and there was a flood of engagements for e-business planning, e-business incubation, VC funding proposals, and so on, riding on the e-commerce wave.

While I was trained in top ERP products and supply chain consulting, in a big-5 consulting organization, we focused on meeting the vision of the engagements, aligning our involvement to steering the program, and having a partner organization to actually implement ERP products. Driven with the desire to involve deeper in IT, in early 2000, I moved to IT service provider industry.

In this chapter, I will discuss the following:

- Shifts I see
- What a digital age consultant would look like
- How I vision the future of the consulting industry
- What would I do differently if I get back into consulting

Digital driving a shift in the way consulting worked

The world of consulting services once showed immunity from the economic downturn and the technological disruptions. The future of consulting is *redefined* in the current agile, modular, collaborative, and *digitally disruptive* era.

Digital transformation is making the consulting firms rethink their models and services to better cater to client needs. Today lines between business and IT have blurred — customer experience, agile/continuous integration/DevOps, social media, mobile and channels, analytics, and cloud are leading the paradigm shift in consulting.

Digital revolution has brought IT departments — development, testing, operations, and business departments — supply chain, ERP, BPM, and e-commerce together to work as one team. A new niche and independent breed of consulting firms and many a start-up digital consulting businesses have emerged that are challenging the market share dominance of the large consulting firms.

The digital age consultant

As the market moves toward customer experience-based services, organizations are looking for the *do it all* category of consultants. As the business grows and transforms, companies are also not certain on the best approach and way forward. This makes a consultant's role all the more important and in demand. The companies want to rely on the consultants' expertise not only for defining business strategy but for end-to-end solution advisory.

Expectations from the consultants is to be more adaptive and delivery-oriented with the following key drivers:

- **Complete Integration**: Consultants are no more expected to play the role of an external advisor. Consultants are expected to be part of the complete business life cycle with both the strategic and implementation know-how.

- **Faster Delivery**: Projects have shorter time span and are more iterative. Consultants are expected to align to this pace of business and deliver more tangible outcomes on the go. Customers expect omni-commerce to deliver completely integrated anytime anywhere solutions. Consultants are expected to drive change management, which is becoming very critical to adapt to speed and benefit from the incremental change.

- **Knowledge of the customer**: Consultants are required to have an in-depth knowledge of the end customer and leverage that to customize changes to the approach and deliver better business results. The businesses are relying more and more on the consultants' expertise of knowing the market trends and statistically forecasting customer expectations.

Future of consulting

The expectations from technology consultants have already started to change and moving towards customer experience delivery and niche areas such as analytics, big data, artificial intelligence, devices, and data security. The demand for consultants is on the rise, and more frequent changes in the industry would benefit consulting industry with an increased demand.

Emerging trends that will define the next round of change in technology consulting would be:

- **Asset-based consulting**: This trend is analytics and predictive technology driven. It encompasses ideas, methodologies, frameworks, and IPs together to deliver consulting services through packaged products and tools. Industrialized consulting services that align with pre-defined solutions and are data driven will be delivered in this fashion. This approach will ensure not reinventing the wheel and deliver considerable savings in terms of time and money.

- **Collaborative consulting**: In the digital and agile era, the appetite for large transformational projects is shrinking and there is a growing preference for more iterative and new technology driven projects. Multi-skilled and virtual teams are coming to the fore. The consulting teams will have to work across departments and throughout the project life cycle. The teams will constitute multispecialty *T-shaped* consultants working from remote locations and connected through digital channels.

- **Specialized consulting**: Currently, cloud migration and legacy modernization projects are consuming good number of technical consultants; five years from now the demand for technical consultants will diminish. The demand will move towards consultants with technology, industry, customer, and geographical knowledge. Consultants will be required to focus more on agile, DevOps, data security, and customer experience related engagements.

- **Quality Assurance Consulting**: As organizations will adopt DevOps, it will significantly change the role of **Quality Assurance (QA)**. The role of QA in the digital world will be to assure business outcomes and to ensure the right level of customer value. These two aspects will drive the QA strategy for any project or program. The requirement moves from mere testers to quality consultants. Consultants will have to focus on continuous quality and clear understanding of priorities. Potential risks to customer value and business performance will need to be addressed by preventing defects that might choke the continuous integration process. Reusable and industry-tested frameworks and approaches such as **Quality Blueprinting (QBP)** tailored for digital engagements, will enable quality consultants to be agile and deliver ahead of competition.

What would I do differently as a consultant now?

While I moved from consulting to IT Services over 16 years ago, all along, I have closely observed the evolution of the management consulting industry and often vision the future of the consulting industry. I ask myself, what is that one thing that I would do differently if I were a consultant once again?

During all my years of consulting, I saw consulting engagements, the Kick-off, Planning, Analysis and Design, Report Back, and Execution phases. While our engagements involved working closely with clients in the kick-off and fact gathering stages, working with clients diminished in the analysis and design phases. Often the report back/recommendation phase was with the CXO level. Often the stakeholders whose inputs were taken at initial phases found themselves eliminated from the entire process.

If I were to redo the consulting methods again, I will do the following.

Engage with my clients more through the life cycle

In today's digital world, the need for transparency across consulting phases is very high.

- Clients would better prefer those consultants who align and closely work with their businesses with transparency

- Discretionary spends are limited and scrutinized, there won't be too many big-ticket consulting engagements

- Information is more open, there would be fewer buyers of *black-box* insights

I would involve the stakeholders who provided initial inputs to validate the solution/recommendations. These stakeholders are key to the success during execution, even if the solution has considered all their inputs, their buy-in is very important.

Don't drop a bomb of travel costs

Best consultants are not always in the same location. Traditionally, the consulting industry has seen high travel costs associated. While travels are still essential, technologies such as Skype, GoogleDoc, Microsoft Lync, and GoToMeeting, have offered virtual collaboration at a low cost and have changed the way consultants operate. Clients are fine with the consultants operating remotely and connecting through electronic media, rather than make flying visits only for the meetings.

Solving the consultant utilization problem with Crowd-Source

Consulting firms are often pre-occupied with *utilization* issues. Bringing learning from IT services industry where billable utilization has been in a range of 90% (as against 60-70% in consulting industry), I believe the consulting industry can benefit from core/flex. The consulting industry can leverage a professional *crowd* of freelancers, for the flex, retaining core of professionals who have a partner level client relationship along with consulting methods expertise.

There could be an argument that this model would suffer quality. In today's digital age, every consultant who has served engagement could get transparent virtual reviews to solve this problem.

Another argument could be the very premise of the consulting industry, *the trusted advisor/partner*. Today clients care more for deep expertise, the consulting firms need to bring the best expertise to table, rather than trying to protect turf only through internal talent.

Flexible operating model of consulting firms

The consulting firms traditionally had industry verticals (Manufacturing/ Retailing/Distribution, Banking), and core practices, for example, Business Process Improvement, Information technology, ERP, and Supply Chain. I have seen many changing operating models during my stint: vertically led, practice led, and so on.

Learning from my IT services experience, the consulting firms of future could be based on *Network Model* to bring the best of various competencies into the engagement. Such a model can also easily leverage external *crowd/freelance* resources.

Conclusion

Considering the paradigm shift industry is seeing in adapting to digital evolution, the need for support from consulting partners would see a rise. To deliver industry expectations, consulting firms need to adapt as per market requirements, expand their horizons, build reusable assets and garner expertise, and niche skill sets. Digital revolution has reached the doors of consulting and firms need to do a seismic shift from traditional to the continuous, collaborative, and comprehensive way of consulting.

44
Future of Testing in the Digital World

This chapter has been written based on the queries received from the testing community. Software Testing has
been evolving since the dawn of computing as a science, an art, and a profession.

The testing discipline too has evolved fast. Regardless of the changes in the technologies and **Information Technology** (IT) landscape, testing has continued to remain the focus areas for organizations, more so in today's digital world, where the cost of failure is high.

Before one makes an attempt to chart out the future of testing in the next decade, it will be good to summarize the technologies of tomorrow that the testing discipline needs to cater to.

Key technology trends that would shape the future of Information Technology

In this section, we will present the following five key technology trends:

- Pervasive technologies and predictive analytics for customer experience
- Cognitive Intelligence in connected autonomous vehicles
- Multi-channel customer connect and wearable technologies
- Dis-intermediation eliminating middlemen
- Changing workplace of the future with the arrival of robots

Pervasive technologies and predictive analytics for customer experience

Pervasive technologies deal with the flow of information between the built-in environment and its occupants. The environment is rich with information that can be utilized to enhance the quality of our work and life. Some basic examples such as customized deals in shopping malls based on geolocalization and buying pattern and traffic alert based on the route taken to the office everyday.

Even **Connected Autonomous Vehicles (CAV)** are good examples of pervasive technologies and predictive analytics as they interact with their environment and based on some specific triggers, they predict the outcome of the events and perform appropriately as shown in the following diagram:

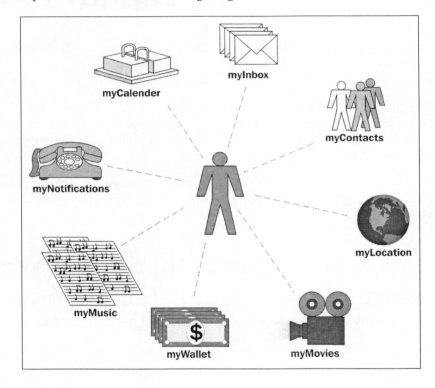

Cognitive Intelligence in Connected Autonomous Vehicle (CAV)

Connected vehicles use different communication technologies to communicate with the driver, other cars on the road (**Vehicle-to-Vehicle (V2V)**), roadside infrastructure (**Vehicle-to-Infrastructure (V2I)**), and the *cloud*.

Autonomous vehicles are those in which the operation of the vehicle occurs without direct driver input to control the steering, acceleration, and braking, and are designed so that the driver is not expected to constantly monitor the roadway while operating in a self-driving mode.

CAV comes with in-built cognitive intelligence and predictive analysis as it has to distinguish between various types of objects on the road, for example, pedestrians, cyclists, and other cars, and take a decision on steering past, acceleration, deceleration, or braking accordingly. The CAV features will improve road safety, enhance the driving experience, reduce the potential for traffic jams, and improve the traffic flow. Take a look at the following image:

Multi-channel customer connect – wearable technology

Wearable technology or fashion electronics are clothing and accessories, comprising a computer and advanced electronic technologies. The designs often incorporate practical functions and features.

Wearable devices are part of the network of physical objects or *things* embedded with electronics, software, sensors, and connectivity to enable objects to exchange data with a manufacturer, operator, and/or other connected devices, without requiring human intervention.

There is a huge application of wearable technology in the personal computing, entertainment and gaming, and e-health sectors:

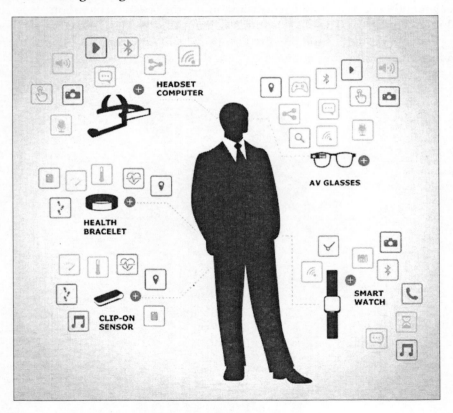

Disintermediation – business platform to connect new partners

Disintermediation platforms are removing intermediaries from a supply chain in connection with a transaction or a series of transactions. In order to decrease the cost of servicing customers, traditional distribution channels, which had some type of intermediate companies such as distributors, wholesalers, brokers, or agents, are now dealing with every customer directly or via the Internet.

Some basic examples are e-commerce platforms, such as Flipkart and Amazon, which source products directly from the manufacturer. Other examples are reselling platforms, such as OLX, which connects the buyer and seller directly enabling the successful transaction.

ITC's e-Choupal has completely removed middlemen and benefitted a huge number of Indian farmers, who can sell their produce at a much better price. Refer to the following image:

Changing workplaces of future – Robotic Process Automation (RPA)

In **Robotic Process Automation (RPA)**, software *robot* replicates the low-skilled actions of humans such as entering data into an **Enterprise Resource Planning (ERP)** platform or follow a set of repetitive processes. RPA software can be configured to capture and interpret the actions of their existing applications used in a variety of business processes. Once the software has been trained to grasp certain processes, it can automatically manipulate data, communicate with other systems, and process transactions as needed. Take a look at the following image:

Testing considerations for new technologies

How are we going to test these new technologies? Is it going to be tricky or just a cakewalk? Let's try to find out the testing considerations for each of these new technologies.

Pervasive technologies and predictive analytics

Testing for pervasive technologies and predictive analytics will have three basic components:

- Business analytics testing on the huge amount of information gathered from the environment
- Thorough testing of the prediction model for extensive coverage of test scenarios
- Testing of the adopted **Near Field Communication (NFC)** technology

Cognitive intelligence – Connected Autonomous Vehicle (CAV)

During testing of CAV, the two most critical factors are cognitive intelligence of the prediction model and response time. While the software onboard will be responsible for predicting the next move of the other objects on the road, the hardware will be responsible for performing the required action within a fraction of a second.

Along with basic connectivity testing, thorough testing of the prediction logic and performance testing of the hardware response time will be of prime importance.

Multi-channel customer connect – wearable technology

Wearable technology primarily consists of sensors and IoT. The testing of wearable technology will primarily focus on testing the sensors and the information captured by them.

Testing the connectivity and internet protocols should also be part of the testing consideration.

Disintermediation – business platform

During testing of a business platform for disintermediation, knowledge of the end-to-end business scenario and process flow is very important. Therefore, the testers have to be savvy with domain understanding as well as the technology used to realize the platform.

Also, from the end-user testing perspective, crowd testing can be a viable choice for all these business platforms.

Changing workplaces of the future – robotic process automation

Robotic process automation is going to change the way we do testing and test automation today. The software components of RPA should be tested the way we test any software component. However, instead of a traditional waterfall, it will be more inclined toward agile, **Extreme Programming (XP)**, **Test-Driven Development (TDD)**, or **Behavior-Driven Development (BDD)**. Having **System Development Engineers in Test (SDET)** in the testing team rather than pure career testers should also help test the RPA.

Conclusion

With the advent of new technologies, the basic testing process and methodology will not change significantly; but at the same time, as these new technologies are evolving and the test basis is ever changing, the traditional waterfall model will give way to more flexible methodologies such as agile, TDD, BDD, and micro-services architecture.

Looking ahead in the future, testing will be more tools-oriented; even the automation scripts will be created by robotic software. Testers also need to upgrade their skills from pure, independent career testers to a more holistic skillset from the technology and business perspective. Eventually, they will have to wear multiple hats because apart from their testing job they have to perform troubleshooting and if needed, coding as well.

45
Future of Testing – Career Opportunities

Software testing as an independent discipline was born nearly two decades ago. There once was a time when IT professionals had to be convinced that testing could be a career; many people thought software development careers were more attractive and that testing meant a manual, monotonous job. However, testing and **Quality Assurance (QA)** as careers have evolved over the years and these myths have since been shaken. Testing and QA careers are rewarding and challenging, like other fields in the IT industry.

This chapter discusses the various opportunities and careers in software testing and QA, career paths, and how to enrich your career in this field. IT veterans and young professionals alike have found their place in the QA and testing world.

Currently, close to 50% of the global testing outsourced work is carried out in India. The size of the testing market is estimated at $40 billion, with 40% of it labeled as *specialized* testing (done by independent testers) against 60% traditional testing (embedded in the development life cycle). The specialized testing share is continually on the rise in line with advancements in software development life cycles, the movement towards DevOps and agile, and continuous testing.

Career options in testing services

Testing professionals can choose from various career paths—technical, architect, consulting, and project management—to move forward in their careers. The **Social media, Mobility, Analytics, and Cloud (SMAC)** world today has made QA even more important. The cost of failure in the digital world today is very high, particularly when one includes the reputational damages, which have made robust QA processes essential. The agile and DevOps world has not eliminated the need for testing; rather, such testing is carried out in sprints, with increased sprints driving the need for more testing and automation. The testing profession has continued to adapt to the rapidly changing needs of dynamic business and the various development methodologies used.

Practitioners in testing services can progress their careers by doing the following:

- Cultivating knowledge in a diverse set of testing solutions, processes, tools, methods, architectures, and disciplines.

- Applying industry expertise and domain-specific knowledge.

- Navigating any one of the four peaks by acquiring breadth and depth in core capabilities.

- Enhancing engagement experiences and undertaking training and mentoring in order to progress to the executive level. Refer to the following diagram:

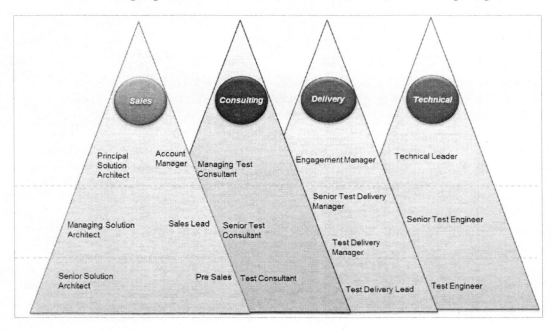

The majority of testing services practitioners are in the technical peak, although career paths are available in each of the four peaks. Practitioners grow core testing skills and capabilities as they progress. Typically, practitioners can decide on a career path in one of the four peaks.

Typical roles in testing services

Testing services practitioners come from a variety of backgrounds. Typical job roles that a testing services practitioner may have today or in the future can include the following:

- Test Specialist
- Test Architect
- Technical Team Leader
- Test Consultant
- Test Manager

Refer to the following diagram for a more detailed explanation:

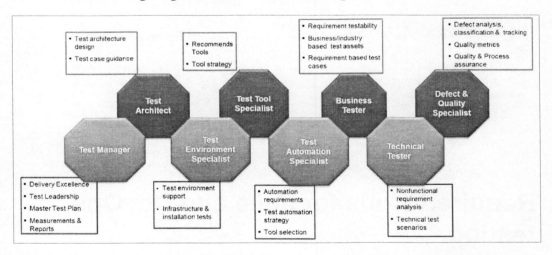

The testing services skill sets include test consulting, test management, planning, execution, test environment, data management, defect management, automation tools comparison and selection, test automation architecting, security testing, performance, and capacity management.

The importance of industry and domain, technology and tools, and process skills in testing careers

Testing careers can leverage domain and analytical skills, process, technical knowledge, technology, tool skills, communication, and soft skills. Above all, attitude, flexibility, and learnability are some of the most desired skills for test professionals. The following diagram indicates the plethora of industry and domains and technology skills one can choose from in order to specialize in their testing career path at providers such as Capgemini:

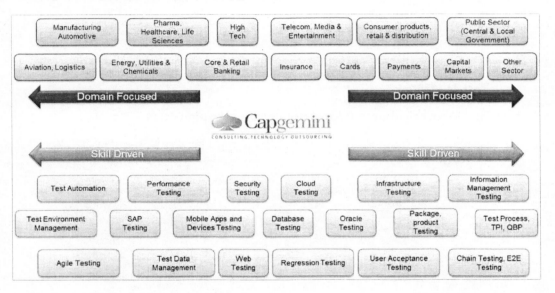

Required skills for agile and DevOps testing

The WQR 2016 surveyed the agile and DevOps skills needed and an organization's readiness with these skills. As per WQR 2016, the testing skills which would see a higher demand in the evolving world of agile and DevOps include test strategy and design skills, test environment virtualization, and non-functional testing (performance, security). Refer to the following diagram:

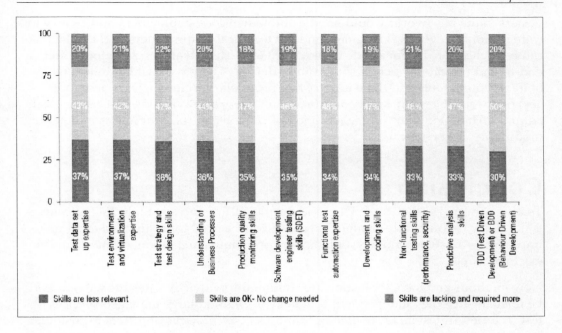

Skills are less relevant				Skills are OK- No change needed				Skills are lacking and required more			

New breed of testers in DevOps

DevOps allows development and infrastructure operations work hand-in-hand and has removed the boundaries of development having to complete a full life cycle for the changes to be deployed. The DevOps approach encourages the developers to understand the testers' job and testers to understand the developer's job. So, what does DevOps have in store for testing careers? Would testers seize to exist?

Testers have evolved over different eras and have moved away from manual black box testing to automation. DevOps is yet another shift that testers are coming to grapple with. Testers would adapt to this shift and fit in. The new testing skills would involve not only test automation, but also unit testing, test-driven development, Infrastructure Automation, and API testing as a part of DevOps. So it is going to be an enriching and exciting career ahead for testers.

Testers need to extend their automation skills into Infrastructure automation for application deployment. Infrastructure automation tools provide a DSL (a simpler higher level language) for dealing with infrastructure. Infrastructure automation scripts are declarative at a high level. Some of the popular tools include Jenkins, Chef, Puppet from Puppetlabs, Ansible, IBM Urbancode, and Electric-flow from Electric Cloud. Using these tools, one adapts the notion of coding on infrastructure and takes a step closer to DevOps. Boundaries between coders and deployers are blurring.

Testers in the new world would handle automated code deployment and be able to code in simple high-level language and not technical scripts coders use. Deployment can be orchestrated from a code deployment tool. The advantage such tools offer is end-to-end traceability across source and artefacts. There is a vast landscape now of deployment tools and there is no risk of proprietary technologies. These tools also offer reusable, community authored, and peer-reviewed code that can be easily adapted. These tools encourage adoption of version control, continuous integration, modularity, and reuse.

Conclusion

Testing comprises 30-40% of SDLC and despite all advances in tools, the percentage is not likely to drastically change. There is always a need for testing, whether one implements a new technology, enhances existing implementation, or maintains the existing code!

New methods and tools for testing are continually evolving, so testers will always be relevant—be they independent testers in TCOEs and large managed services test factories, or testers in smaller agile and DevOps projects, or testers to customer development projects with Java, .NET, or testers for enterprise applications such as SAP and Oracle.

Testing is a field that can leverage an individual's multi-faceted skills in business, technical, process, domain, industry, and soft skills.

46

Robotics and Machine Learning Combined with Internet of Things – What Could This Mean for Indian Services Industries

The crash of oil prices and slowdown of China's economy have fetched headlines in the media of late. The subject has encouraged me to understand economic reasons and relate the implications for Indian services industries. It would be good to preempt a discussion on the topic whether what happened to Chinese manufacturing or to Middle East oil industry could repeat for Indian IT? If so, what should India do to prepare itself today to face this future?

Understanding the context – robotics, machine learning, and IoT

You are in the final lap of your early morning dream and the alarm goes off at 6 AM. Suddenly you remember that you forgot to buy milk yesterday and since you have an early morning meeting, it seems that you have to start your day without your cup of steaming coffee. Fortunately, your refrigerator has already ordered milk, based on your regular consumption pattern and available inventory. Also, your alarm clock has already instructed your coffee maker to start brewing your coffee and based on your office timing/meeting schedule, your laptop has instructed your geyser to keep the water in the bathroom at your preferred temperature.

Does it sound like dream or science fiction? Not anymore. With the rapid development in the field of robotics, machine learning, and **Internet of Things (IoT)**, we have all the pieces of technology to make this happen, and it's just a matter of time when these technology pieces will be integrated to transform our way of living.

Robotics deals with programmed machines designed to do labor-intensive work. **Machine learning** is the science of getting computers and machines to function without being programmed to do so. The combination of Robotics and machine learning results in Robots with the capability to do the jobs on their own for example, self-driving cars.

Machine Learning tasks can start with supervised learning, then move to a semi-supervised state, and then unsupervised learning. It basically contains the essence of statistical pattern recognition, parametric/non-parametric algorithms, neural networks, recommender, systems, and so on. machine learning is an advanced state of intelligence—with **Internet of Things (IoT)**, multiple robots can get interconnected.

IoT offers an environment where objects or people have unique identifiers and the ability to transfer data over a network without requiring human-to-human or human-to-computer interaction. As per Gartner, by 2020 there will be over 26 billion connected devices. IoT can be applied to monitoring and capturing data from anything and everything connected to a network, for example, Media, Environmental Monitoring, Infrastructure Management, Manufacturing, Energy Management, Medical and Healthcare Systems, Building and Home Automation, or Transportation.

A thing, in the IoT, can be anything that can be assigned an IP address and has the ability to transfer data over a network, for example, a patient with a heart monitor implant, and other similar devices/objects. IPv6 has offered the capability of assigning unique IP addresses to every atom on the surface of the Earth for many Earths.

What does advancement of technology mean for the Indian economy?

Advancement of IT has been a boon for the Indian economy. 27% of India's workforce deployed in the services sector contribute to 57% of the GDP (compare this with 50% workforce in agriculture contributing to 17% of the GDP and 22% workforce in manufacturing contributing to 26% of the GDP).

How would the advancement of technology impact the GDP? There are two ways to look at this. Currently, the IT work in India has a linear correlation to the number of people deployed. If the same work can be done with smarter machines/robots in India, the GDP would go even further up, keeping the percentage of workforce deployed same or lesser.

Let's discuss any learnings from the global oil price crash and from the slowdown of Chinese manufacturing/the Chinese economy.

Learning from the global oil price crash

I started to analyze what caused the crash of oil prices. Going with the simple demand-supply logic, the reasons could include these:

- Increase in the supply of oil
- Reduced demand for oil

One of the key reasons cited to increased oil supply is Fracking, a technique that extracts more hydrocarbon from the ground that has increased the oil extraction yield, resulting in larger supply of oil, even though the same has caused concerns on environmental damage. At the same time, there has been reduced demand for oil with more and more fuel-efficient cars, plants, and gadgets.

Oil price crash could further aggravate with advances in solar and wind energy production and usage. It is expected that in another 20 years, solar energy that meets 1% energy needs today would meet 100% of the energy needs making energy almost free. Disruptive innovations improve performance multifold at the same time reduce the cost of technology.

Learning from the economic slowdown of China—what caused the slowdown in China?

Many developed countries moved their manufacturing to China boosting the Chinese economy. However, over the years, increased labor and shipping cost reduced the cost advantage. Today, robots have replaced labor in manufacturing, making Chinese manufacturing less competitive. For China to continue its competitive advantage in manufacturing, many Chinese companies have begun to deploy robots in factories. However, this would not solve the shipping cost problems, many developed countries would take back the manufacturing work back to their base and use robots.

Conventional manufacturing space is changing as well, with now increased use of 3D printing. 3D printing could evolve in printers for home that could produce toys and other household goods. Advanced 3D printers may then compete against robots.

Did the above shocks happen all of a sudden or were these predictable? Anyone who can intelligently observe the evolution of technology should have been able to predict the oil price crash or slowdown of the Chinese economy.

Outlook for the the services sector in India – a point of view

The technological advances could have a negative impact on the agricultural sector workforce if machines only replace human labor. Agriculture sector has to use technology to make farming more effective. For example, IoT-enabled sensors on the farmland can perform a soil culture test and take a decision on the amount of fertilizer, manures, and water needed. Results can then be validated with the meteorological data on rainfall and temperature. Such technological advances would help farmers do farming more effectively and efficiently.

The service sector will benefit from this technological boon as robots can be utilized to perform the mundane repetitive jobs, starting from all Level 1 support in customer care centers, teller services in banks, check-ins in airports, waiting services in restaurants, and even coding and testing in the IT industry.

As these robots keep learning on the job due to their machine learning capability, they can perform the job even better than they were initially programmed and eventually develop the decision making skills. The human workforce can be utilized for more complex activities that require emotional intelligence.

If the countries that source IT services from India deploy smarter machines directly, there could be an adverse impact on India. So India has to produce the smart machines itself and program them, to be able to lead the change, rather than be threatened about robots resulting in loss of jobs.

Conclusion

The world is going through a breakthrough technology shift, which can help transform lives. The implications of technological advancement and evolution of nations is a good topic of research. America leads the technology boom and reinvents itself through economic cycles every 30-40 years. The Middle East, once known for oil monopoly is going through instability. More oil producers such as Venezuela would find it uneconomic to produce oil.

China joined the race for manufacturing a few decades back with its cost-effective skilled labor, with global manufacturing finding destination in China — but the country has already seen an economic slowdown.

Recently, India joined this race of manufacturing and industrial output with the *Make in India* initiative by the Government of India. While India is late in the race, being late could have an advantage as well of being the first in adapting to new technology.

India with its large population, strong consumer economy, investment in education, democratic political structure has the potential to lead the change. Robotics and machine learning when combined with IoT offer technological advancement help build a stronger India.

References

Across Chapters – World Quality Report 2016 (Capgemini, Sogeti, HPE):

- www.worldqualityreport.com
- http://ow.ly/9Ja2305zRIy

Chapter 2 – Future of Testing Engagement Models – Are Predictions of increased QA Spends Justified?

- Diego Lo Guidice, Forrester Research *Five Considerations for Shifting Left*: http://servicevirtualization.com/forrester-talks-about-five-considerations-for-shifting-left/

Chapter 3 – The Benefits of Replacing Testing Subcontractors with Managed Testing Services

- Gartner Magic Quadrant (2016) for Application Testing Services: https://www.gartner.com/doc/3527219/magic-quadrant-application-testing-services

Chapter 18 – Service Virtualization as an Enabler of DevOps

- voke Market Snapshot Report 2015 – Service Virtualization: `https://www.vokeinc.com/enterprise-service-virtualization-data.html`

Chapter 30 – Key Considerations in Testing Internet of Things (IOT) Applications

- Gartner – The Internet of Things Installed Base Will Grow to 26 Billion Units By 2020; Dec 2013: `http://www.gartner.com/newsroom/id/2636073`

- Morgan Stanley – 75 Billion Devices Will Be Connected To The Internet Of Things By 2020; Oct 2013: `http://www.businessinsider.in/Morgan-Stanley-75-Billion-Devices-Will-Be-Connected-To-The-Internet-Of-Things-By-2020/articleshow/23426604.cms`

- The Internet of things: Networked objects and smart devices; The Hammersmith Group; Feb 2010: `http://www.theinternetofthings.eu/sites/default/files/Rob%20van%20Kranenburg/networked_objects.pdf`

Chapter 31 – Algorithmic Business – In Need of Model-Based Testing

- Gartner IT Glossary: `http://www.gartner.com/it-glossary/algorithmic-business/`

Chapter 46 – Robotics and Machine Learning Combined with Internet of Things – What could this mean for Indian Services Industries

- Gartner – The Internet of Things Installed Base Will Grow to 26 Billion Units By 2020; Dec 2013: `http://www.gartner.com/newsroom/id/2636073`

Index

entities, FinTech ecosystem
  government 208
  Hi-Tech Firms 208
  traditional firms 208
enumeration 133
environment management automation
  benefits 113
environment management service
  on cloud 91
Ethereum 215
EUC customer journey
  testing considerations 255
Extreme Programming (XP) 296

F

factory 23
failover 147
feedback loop 197
FinTech
  about 207
  services 209, 210
FinTech applications
  testing 210, 211
FinTech ecosystem
  about 207
  entities 208
focus of QA, in supply chain 222, 223
formal governance model 39
Forrester 9
functional testing 193

G

Galen framework 273
Gartner 9
Gherkin
  about 84
  benefits 86
  syntax 84
Gherkin language
  example 85
  syntax 84
global automotive evolution
  business drivers 234

global automotive trends, influence on
    Chinese market
  dealer strategy 235
  OEM strategy 235
  supplier strategy 235
Global Distribution System (GDS) 272
Graphic User Interface (GUI) 123

H

Hadoop Distributed File systems
    (HDFS) 148
hardware bottlenecks 131
Healthcare and Life Sciences
    (H&LS) industry
  about 277
  challenges, in application testing 278
  requisites 278
Hot Spots 136
hybrid QA teams 10

I

IBM automated accessibility tester 130
IBM digital content checker 129
Incident Management 178
Incident Management Team (IMT) 178
Incident Response Team (IRT) 178
industrialization and testing
    centers of excellence
  findings, from World Quality
    Report 2016 15
Industrialize Plateau 12
Information Technology (IT)
  about 289
  key technology trends 289-294
In Home Devices (IHD) 262
Innovate Plateau 13
input 197
International Air Transport
    Association (IATA) 269
Internet Booking Engine (IBE) 272
Internet of Things (IoT) 189, 196, 252, 304
IoT Revolution
  key findings, from World Quality
    Report 2016 191

memory usage 137, 138
thread states 135
Net Promoter Score (NPS) 145
network testing 193
new technologies, in supply
    chain management
  3D printing 221
  analytics and big data 220
  blockchain 221
  cloud computing 221
  FinTech Businesses 220
  Internet of Things (IoT) 221
  smart machines 221
nodes 214

O

obsolete test cases 124
omni-channel retailing 243
on-demand performance testing
  key scenarios 165-168
on-demand performance testing
    environment
  key challenges 164
  solutions 164
on-demand self-service environments
  for performance testing 165
on-demand tester staffing 32
online stores 242
operating models, crowdtesting
  on-demand tester staffing 32
  testing as service 32
Original Equipment Manufacturers
    (OEMs) 235
Orthogonal Array Testing (OAT) 277
Orthogonal Array Testing (OAT) tool
  benefits 280
Orthogonal Array Testing Strategy (OATS)
  benefits 279
  using 279
Outage Management System (OMS) 265
output 197

P

Parasoft Virtualize 119
Patch Management 178
performance analysis 131

performance bottlenecks
  about 131
  comparison, versus identity 133
  constants, enumerating 133
  delayed initialization 134
  excess garbage collection, avoiding 133
  objects, canonicalizing 133
  objects, reusing 132
  pool of objects, managing 132
performance testing 147, 193
performance testing, of Microservices 106
pervasive technologies 295
physical stores 240, 241
pivotal areas, utilities future landscape
  analytics 253
  cloud 252
  integration 253
  mobility 253
  smart systems 253
Platform-as-a-Service (PaaS) 114, 236
platforms, Cognitive Intelligence
  Google DeepMind 203
  IBM Watson 203
  OpenAI 203
plug-in hybrid electric vehicles
    (PHEVs) 265
Point of Sales (PoS) 240
predictive analytics 295
production-like environments 164
PTaaS solution
  benefits 165
  features 165
Puppet 114

Q

QA
  testing transformation drivers 2
  testing transformation focus 2
QA and testing, airline industry
  about 271
  non-functional testing 272
  systems integration testing 272
  testing business rules implementation 272
QA, digital marketing applications
  key validations 171, 172